FIRST 50 MELODIES

YOU SHOULD PLAY ON UKULELE

ISBN 978-1-5400-5061-8

Visit Hal Leonard Online at
www.halleonard.com

Contact us:
Hal Leonard
7777 West Bluemound Road
Milwaukee, WI 53213
Email: info@halleonard.com

In Europe, contact:
Hal Leonard Europe Limited
42 Wigmore Street
Marylebone, London, W1U 2RN
Email: info@halleonardeurope.com

In Australia, contact:
Hal Leonard Australia Pty. Ltd.
4 Lentara Court
Cheltenham, Victoria, 3192 Australia
Email: info@halleonard.com.au

CONTENTS

All My Loving

Words and Music by John Lennon and Paul McCartney

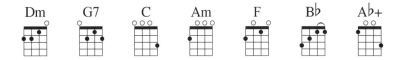

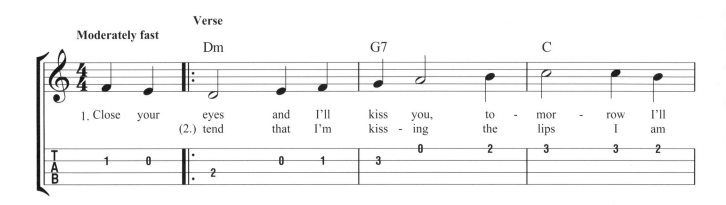

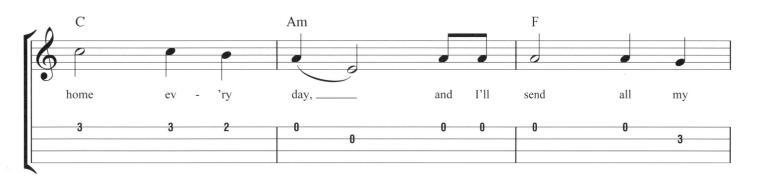

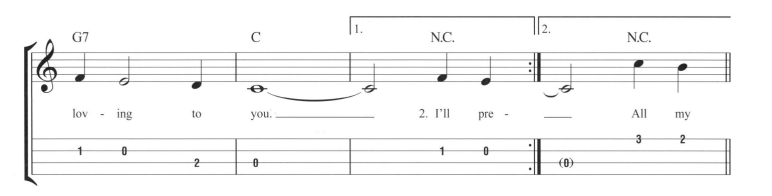

Chorus

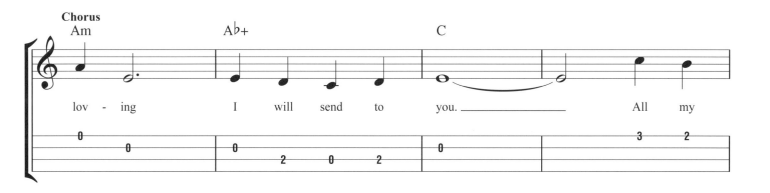

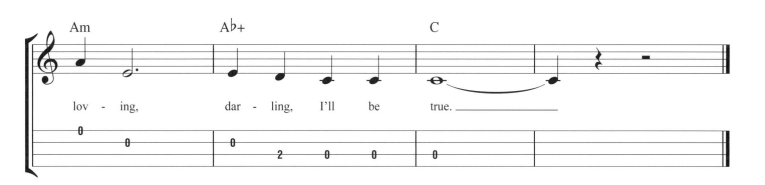

Aloha Oe

Words and Music by Queen Liliuokalani

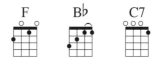

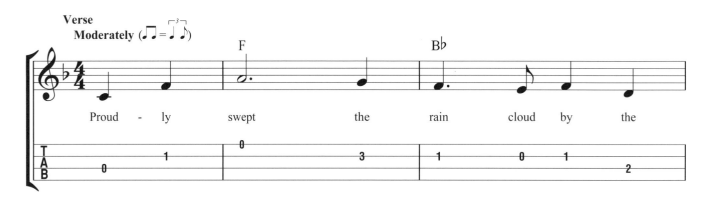

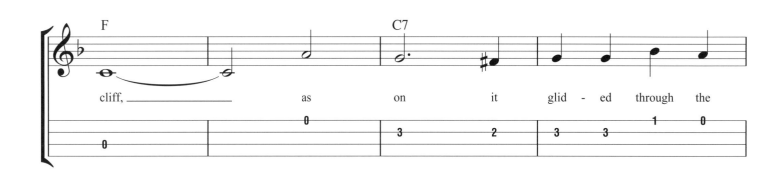

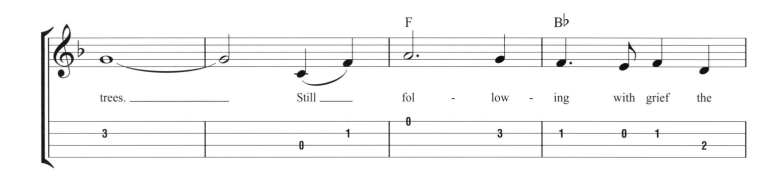

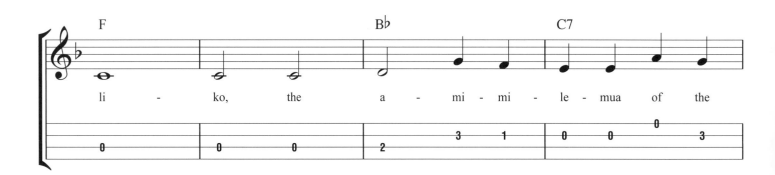

Chorus

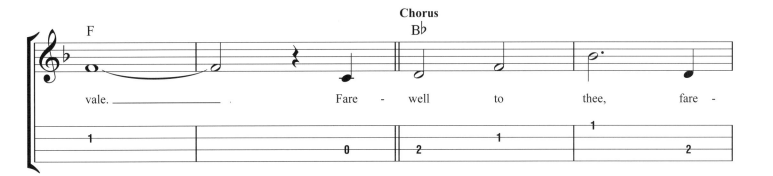

vale. _____ Fare - well to thee, fare -

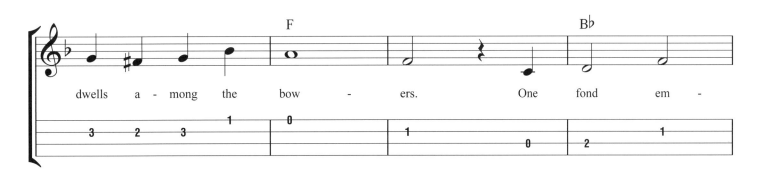

well to thee, thou charm - ing one who

dwells a - mong the bow - ers. One fond em -

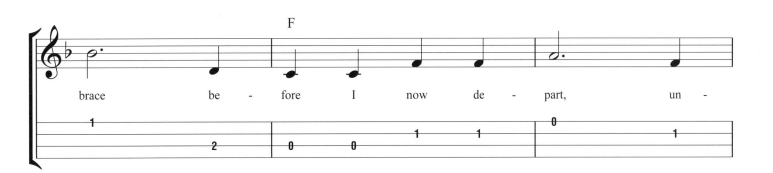

brace be - fore I now de - part, un -

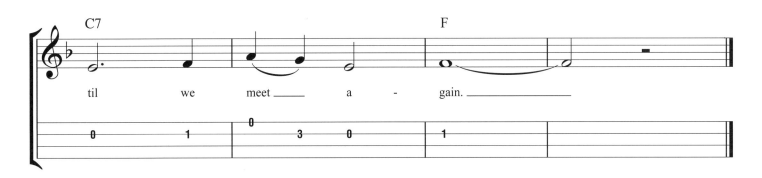

til we meet _____ a - gain. _____

Amazing Grace

Words by John Newton
Traditional American Melody

As Tears Go By

Words and Music by Mick Jagger, Keith Richards and Andrew Loog Oldham

Beautiful Brown Eyes

Traditional

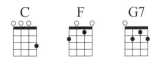

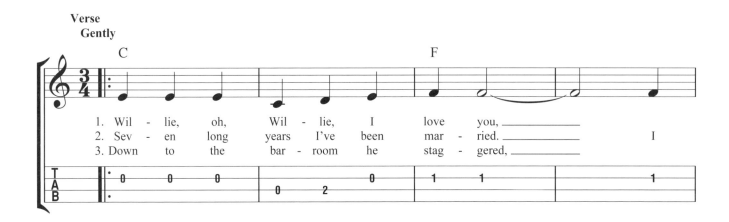

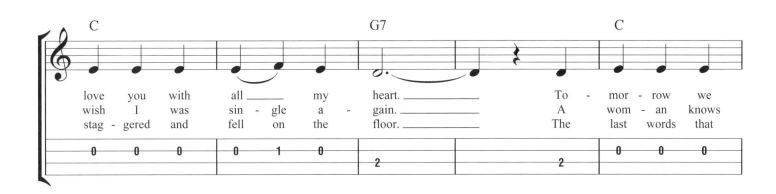

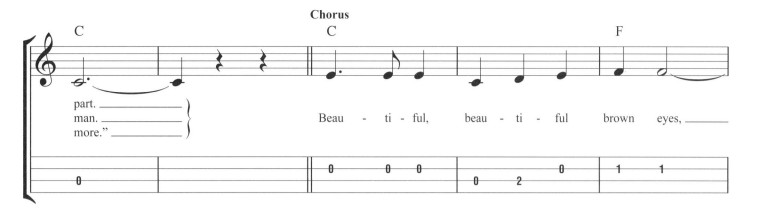

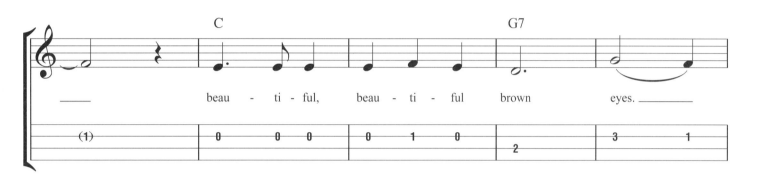

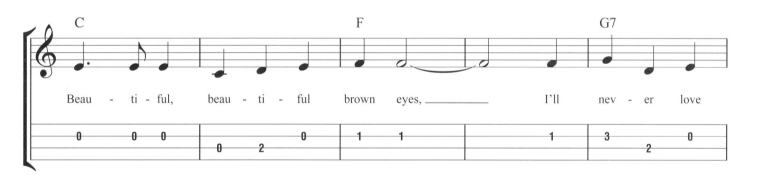

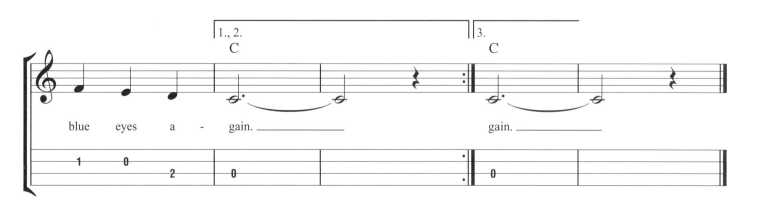

Blue Skies

from BETSY

Words and Music by Irving Berlin

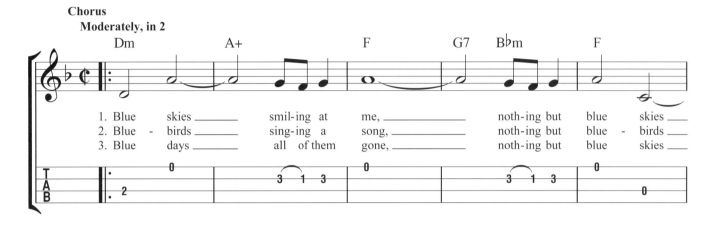

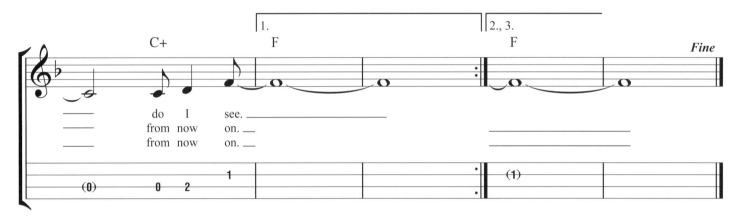

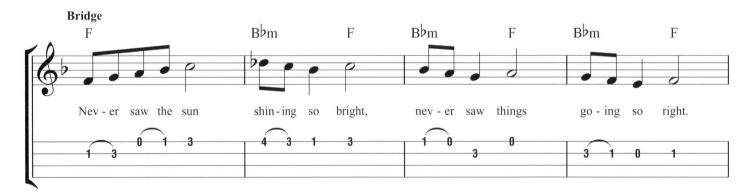

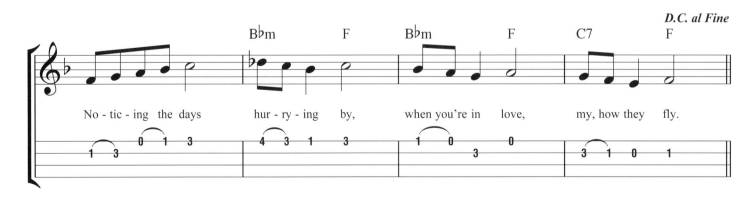

Can't Help Falling in Love

from the Paramount Picture BLUE HAWAII

Words and Music by George David Weiss, Hugo Peretti and Luigi Creatore

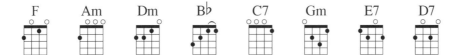

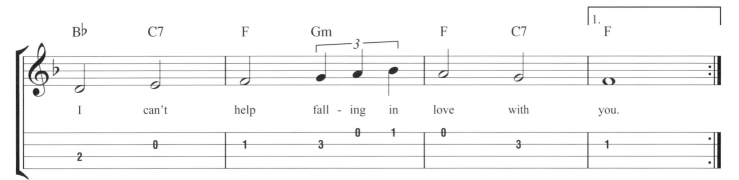

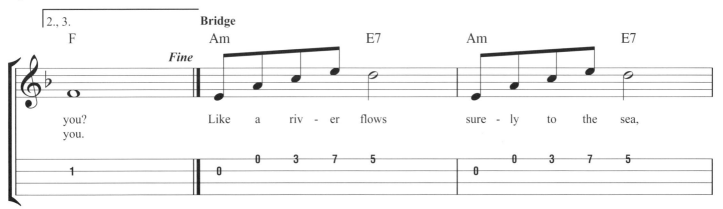

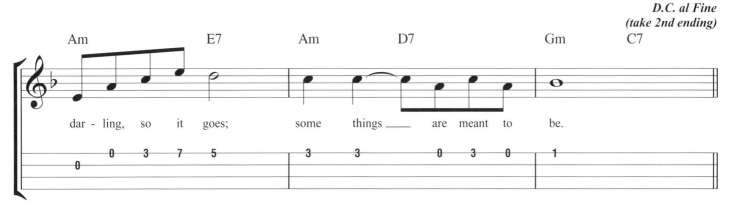

D.C. al Fine
(take 2nd ending)

Bye Bye Love

Words and Music by Felice Bryant and Boudleaux Bryant

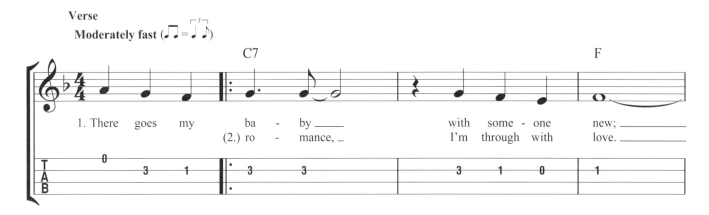

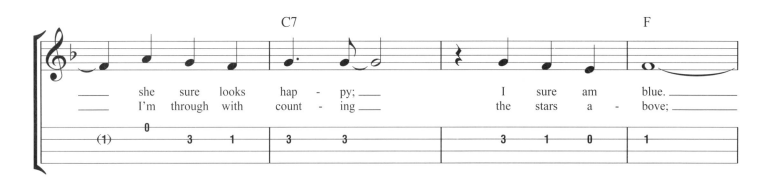

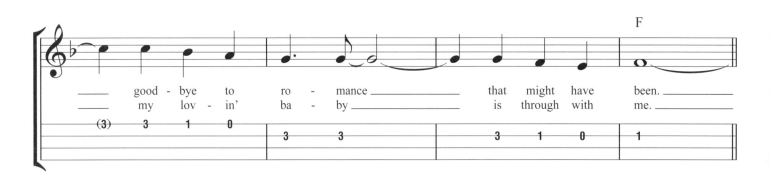

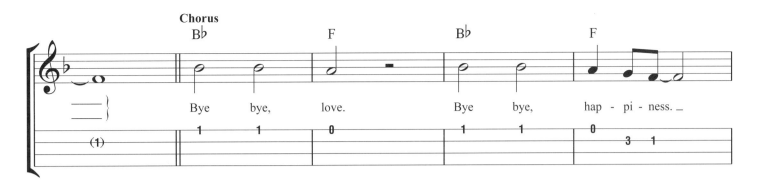

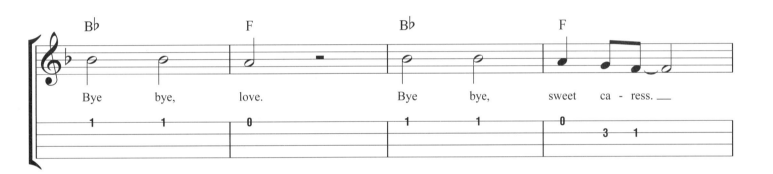

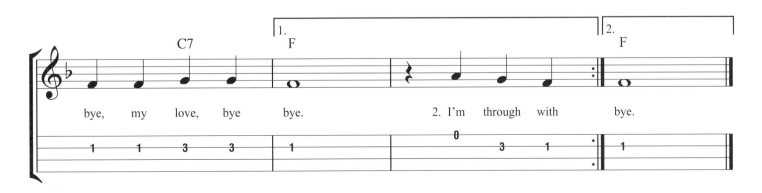

Can You Feel the Love Tonight

from THE LION KING
Music by Elton John
Lyrics by Tim Rice

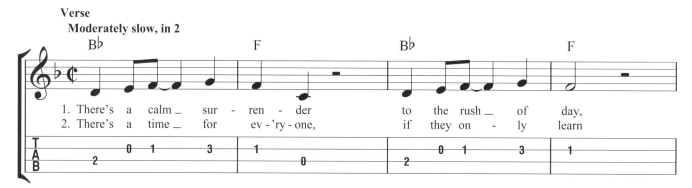

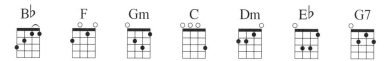

Verse
Moderately slow, in 2

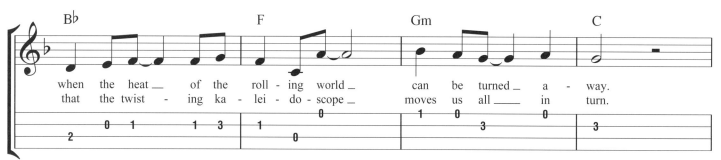

1. There's a calm _ sur-ren-der   to the rush _ of day,
2. There's a time _ for ev-'ry-one,   if they on-ly learn

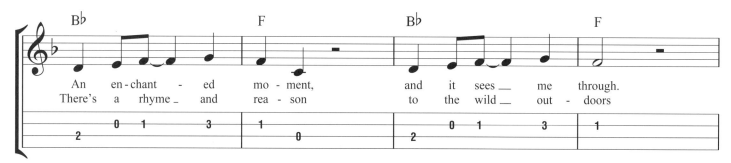

when the heat _ of the roll-ing world _   can be turned _ a-way.
that the twist-ing ka-lei-do-scope _   moves us all _ in turn.

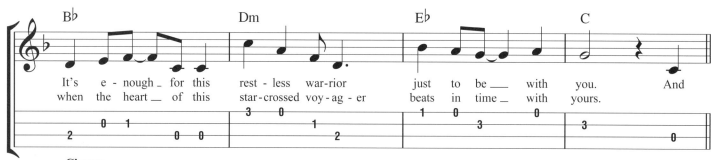

An en-chant-ed   mo-ment,   and it sees _ me through.
There's a rhyme _ and   rea-son   to the wild _ out-doors

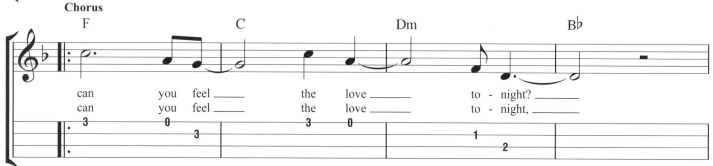

It's e-nough _ for this   rest-less war-rior   just to be _ with you.   And
when the heart _ of this   star-crossed voy-ag-er   beats in time _ with yours.

Chorus

can you feel _____ the love _____ to-night? _____
can you feel _____ the love _____ to-night,

Don't Stop Believin'

Words and Music by Steve Perry, Neal Schon and Jonathan Cain

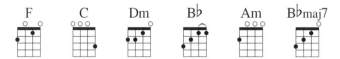

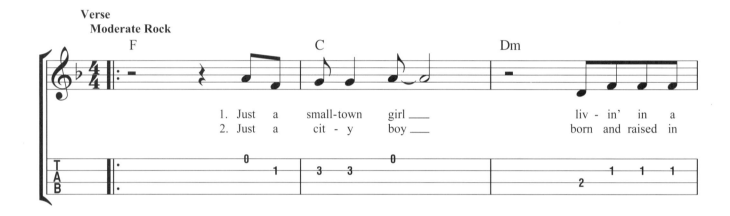

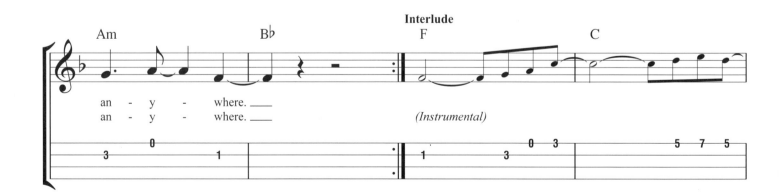

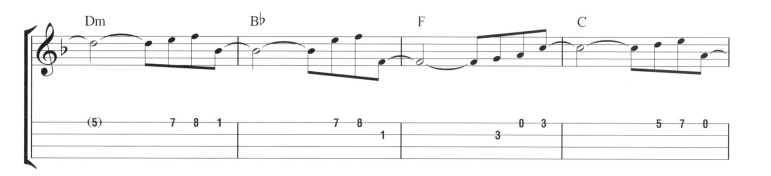

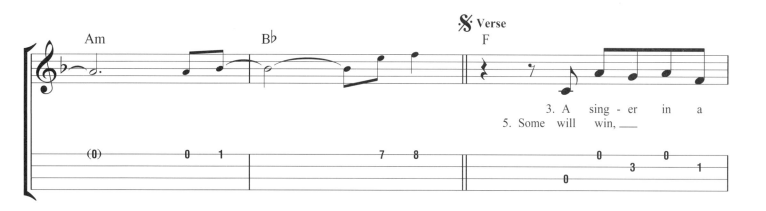

Verse

3. A sing - er in a
5. Some will win, ___

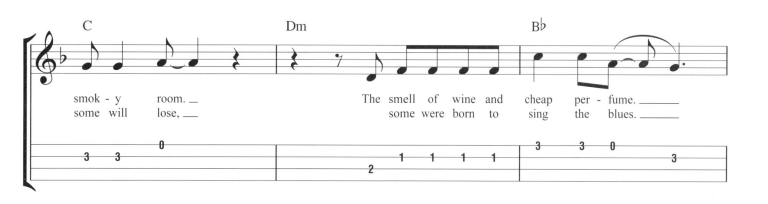

smok - y room. ___
some will lose, ___

The smell of wine and cheap per - fume. _____
some were born to sing the blues. _____

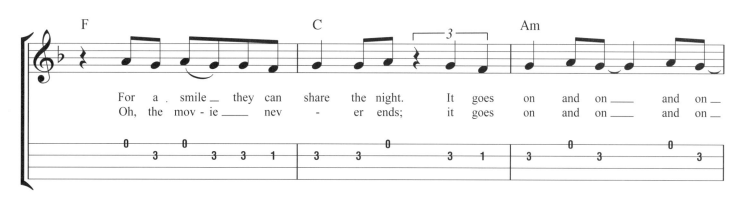

For a smile __ they can share the night. It goes on and on ___ and on _
Oh, the mov - ie ___ nev - er ends; it goes on and on ___ and on _

19

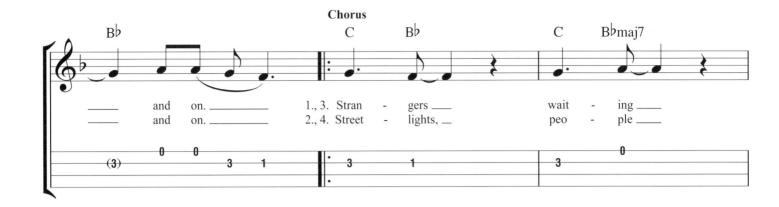

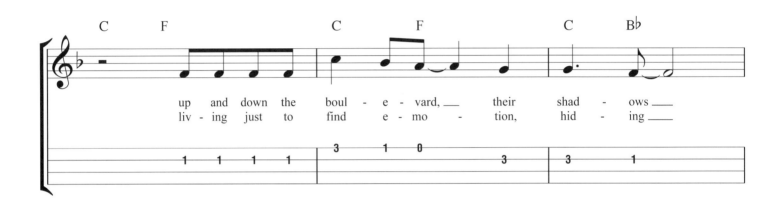

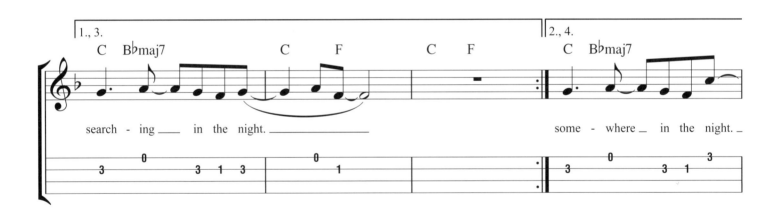

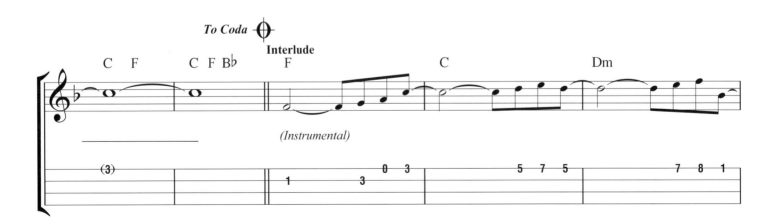

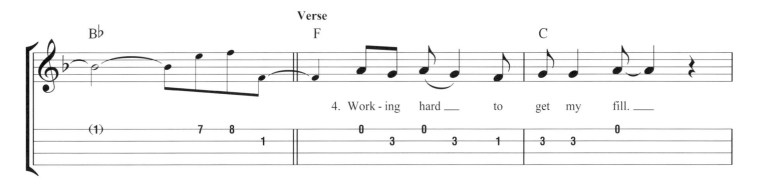

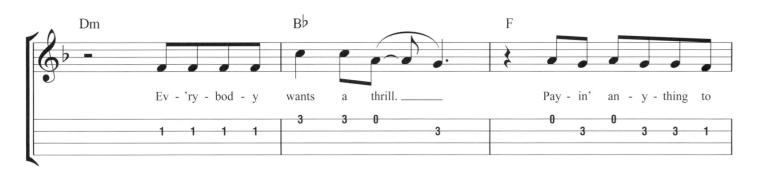

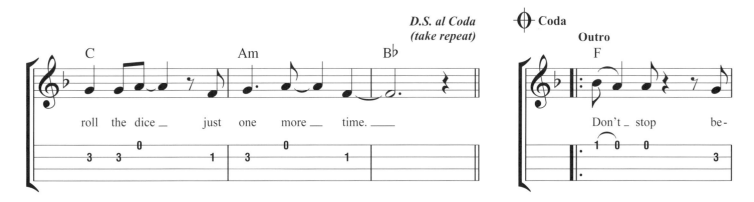

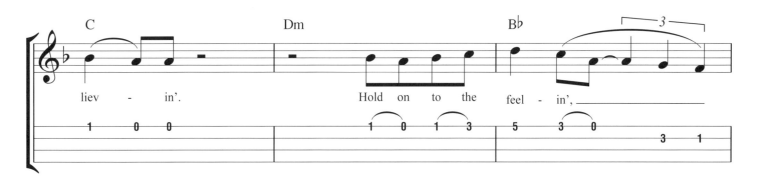

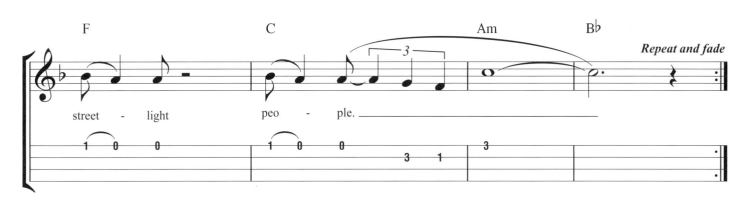

Down in the Valley

Traditional American Folksong

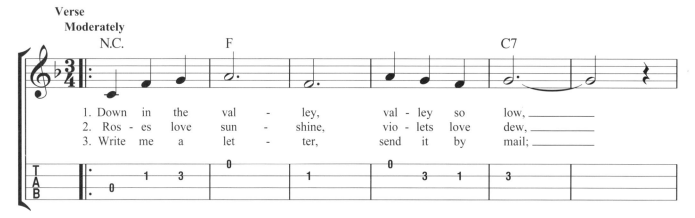

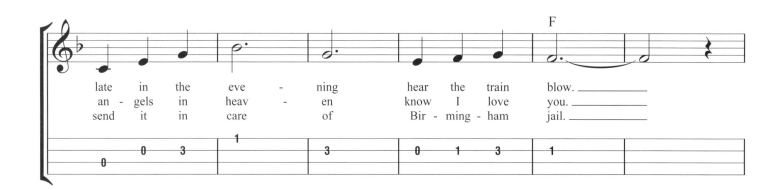

1. Down in the val - ley, val - ley so low, ___
2. Ros - es love sun - shine, vio - lets love dew, ___
3. Write me a let - ter, send it by mail; ___

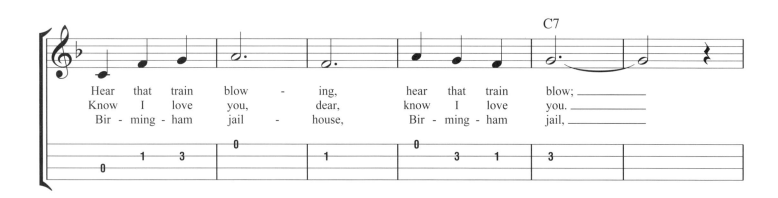

late in the eve - ning hear the train blow. ___
an - gels in heav - en know I love you. ___
send it in care of Bir - ming - ham jail. ___

Hear that train blow - ing, hear that train blow; ___
Know I love you, dear, know I love you. ___
Bir - ming - ham jail - house, Bir - ming - ham jail, ___

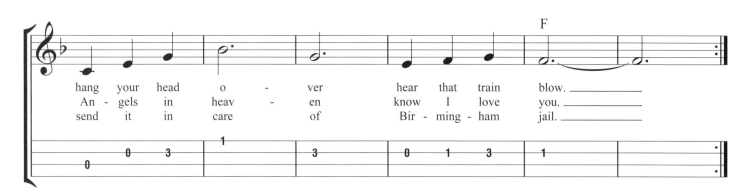

hang your head o - ver hear that train blow. ___
An - gels in heav - en know I love you. ___
send it in care of Bir - ming - ham jail. ___

Edelweiss

from THE SOUND OF MUSIC
Lyrics by Oscar Hammerstein II
Music by Richard Rodgers

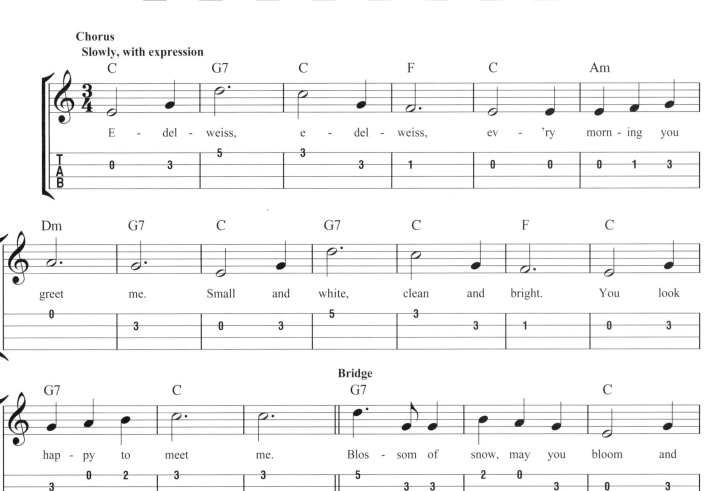

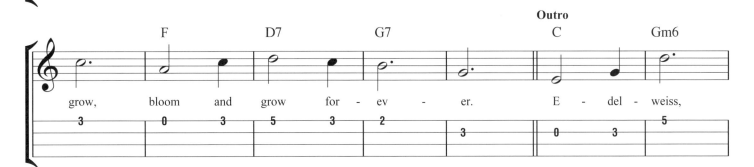

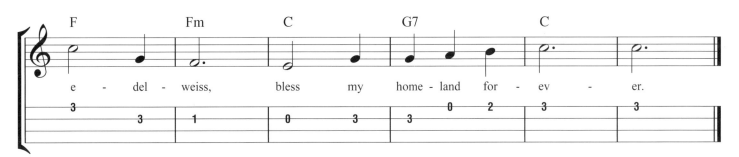

Every Breath You Take

Music and Lyrics by Sting

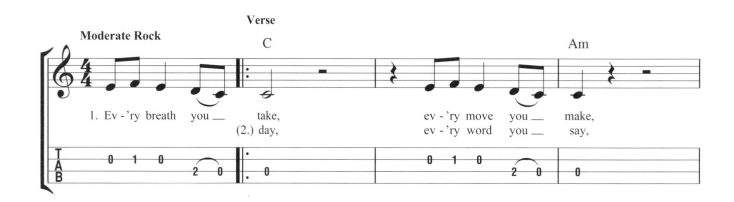

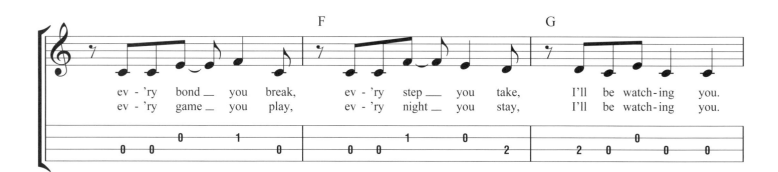

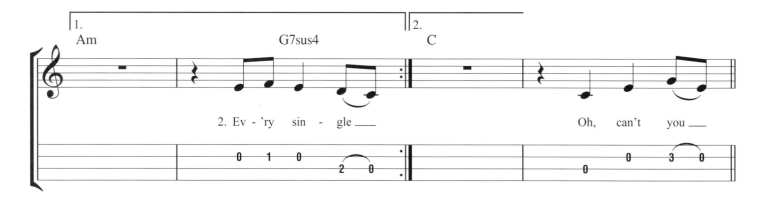

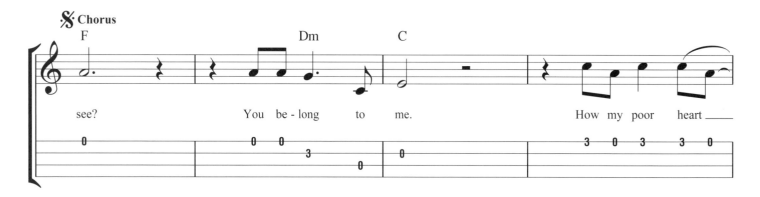

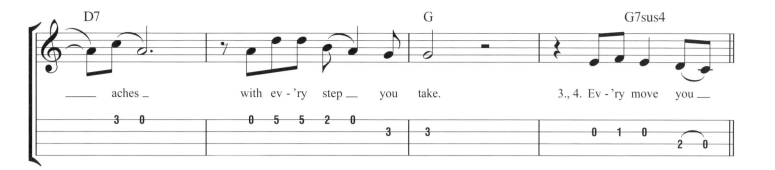

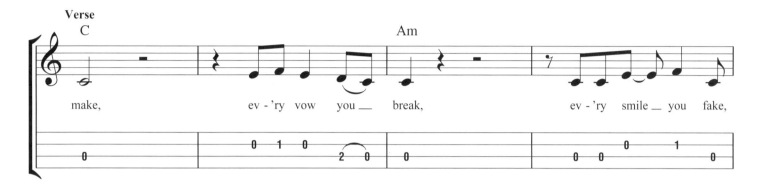

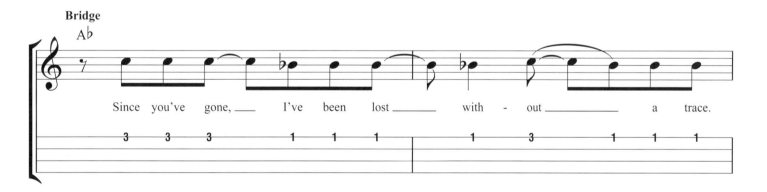

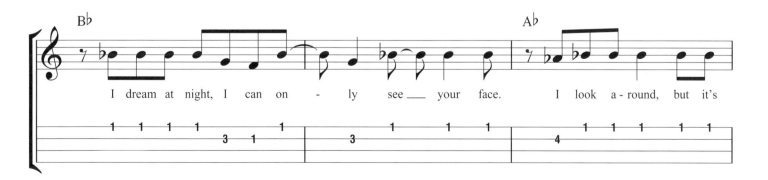

you I can't — re - place. I feel so cold and I long for your — em - brace.

I keep cry - ing, ba - by, ba - by, please. ___

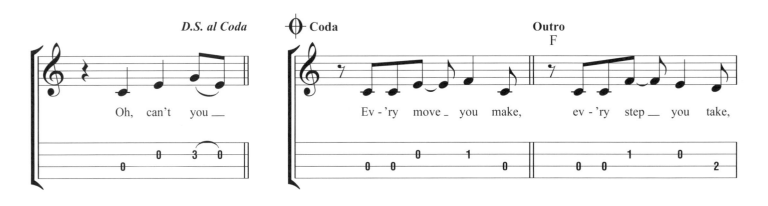

D.S. al Coda

Oh, can't you —

Coda

Outro

Ev - 'ry move — you make, ev - 'ry step — you take,

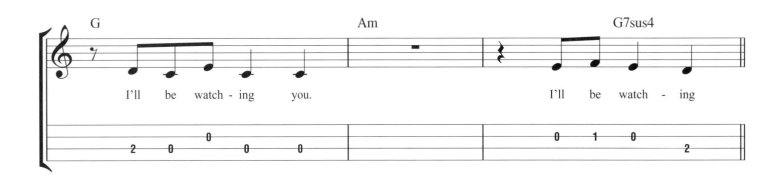

I'll be watch - ing you. I'll be watch - ing

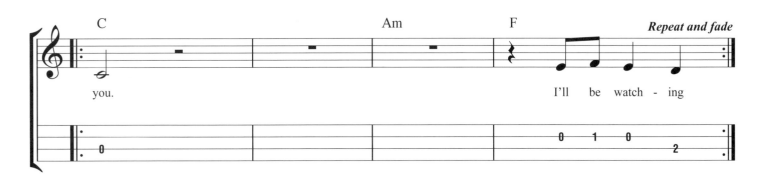

you. I'll be watch - ing

Eight Days a Week

Words and Music by John Lennon and Paul McCartney

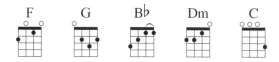

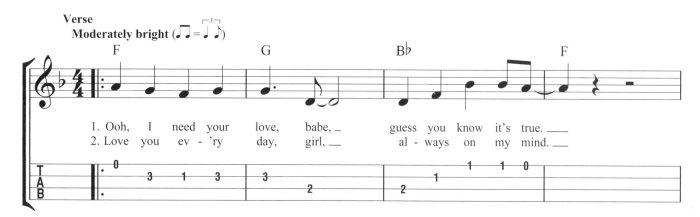

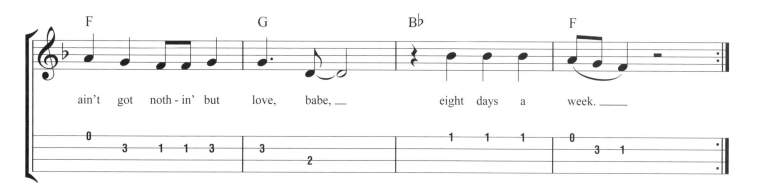

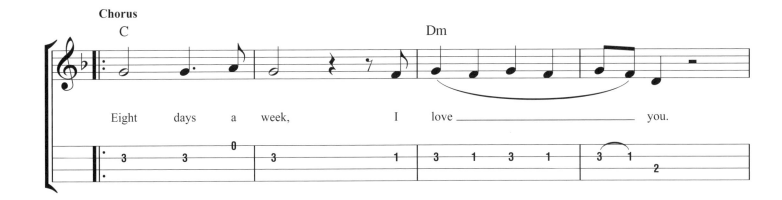

Eight days a week, I love you.

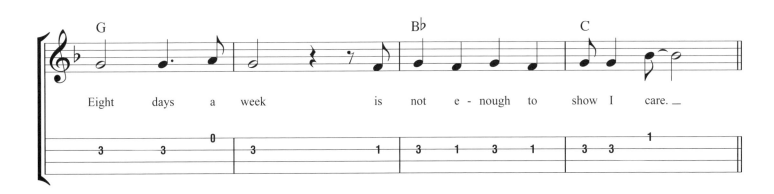

Eight days a week is not e-nough to show I care.

Verse

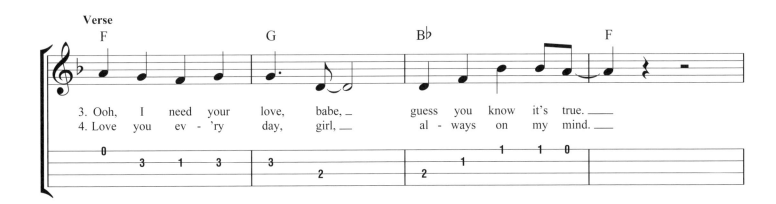

3. Ooh, I need your love, babe, guess you know it's true.
4. Love you ev-'ry day, girl, al-ways on my mind.

Hope you need my love, babe, just like I need you.
One thing I can say, girl, love you all the time.

Pre-Chorus

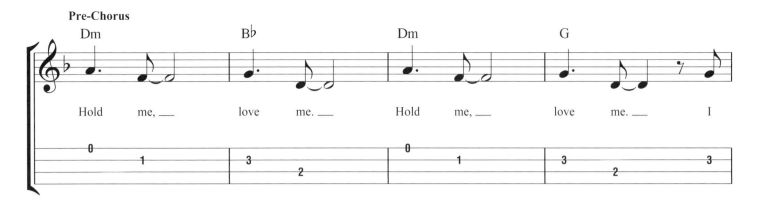

Hold me, __ love me. __ Hold me, __ love me. __ I

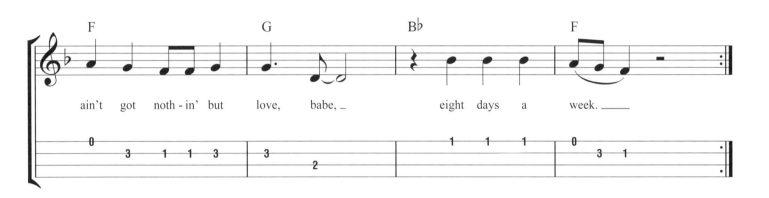

ain't got noth-in' but love, babe, __ eight days a week. _____

Outro

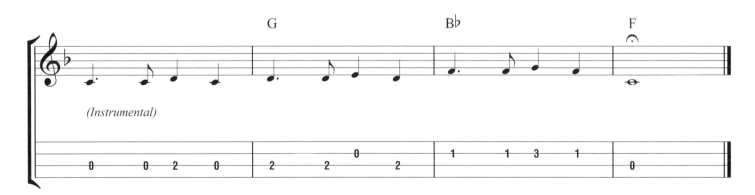

Eight days a week. _____ eight days a week. _____

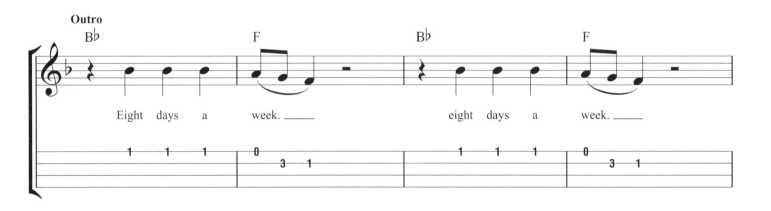

(Instrumental)

Fields of Gold

Music and Lyrics by Sting

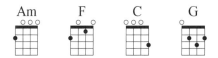

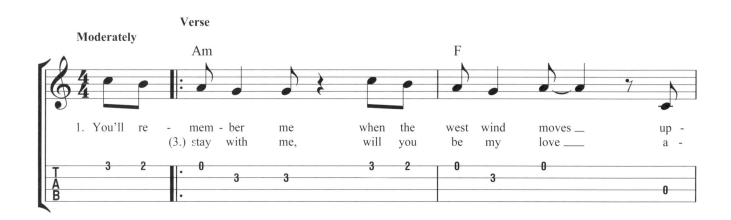

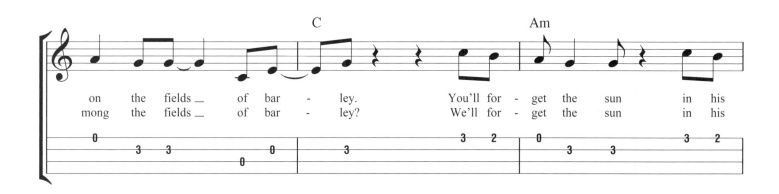

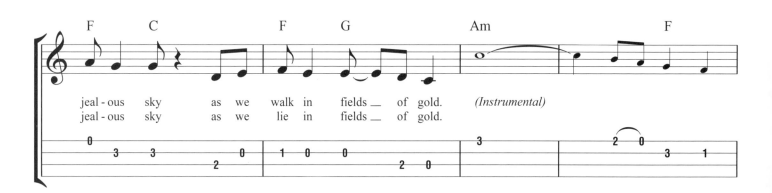

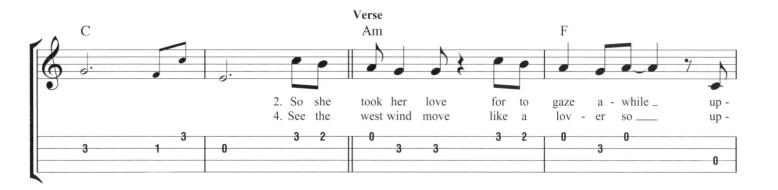

2. So she took her love for to gaze a - while _ up -
4. See the west wind move like a lov - er so ___ up -

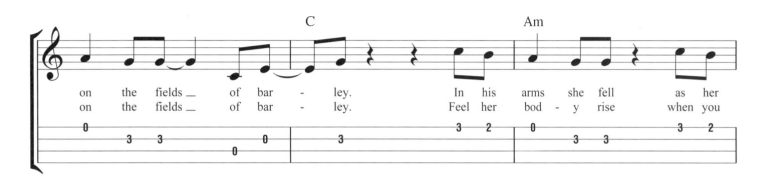

on the fields _ of bar - ley.   In his arms she fell   as her
on the fields _ of bar - ley.   Feel her bod - y rise   when you

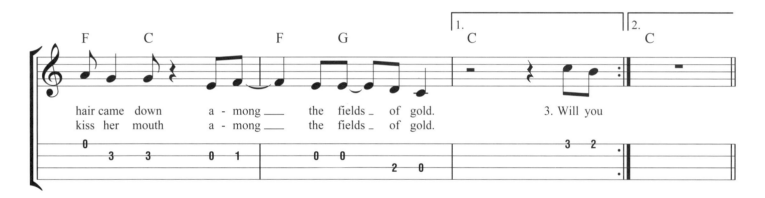

hair came down a - mong ___ the fields _ of gold.   3. Will you
kiss her mouth a - mong ___ the fields _ of gold.

Bridge

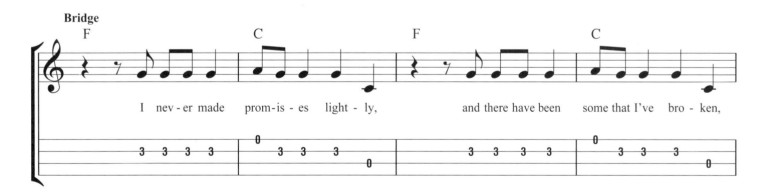

I nev - er made prom-is - es light - ly,   and there have been   some that I've bro - ken,

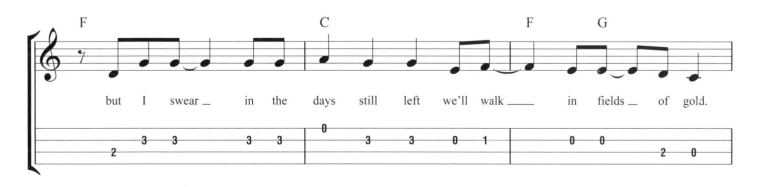

but I swear _ in the days still left we'll walk ___ in fields _ of gold.

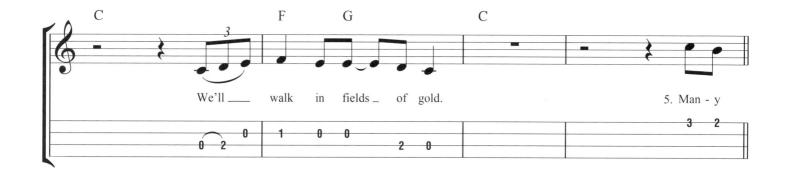

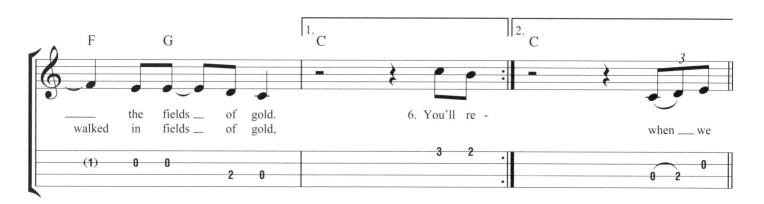

Happy Birthday to You

Words and Music by Mildred J. Hill and Patty S. Hill

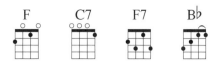

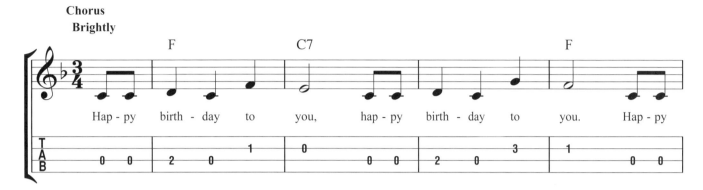

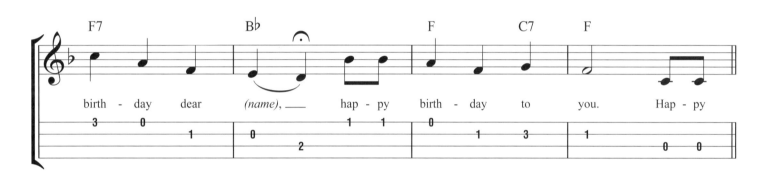

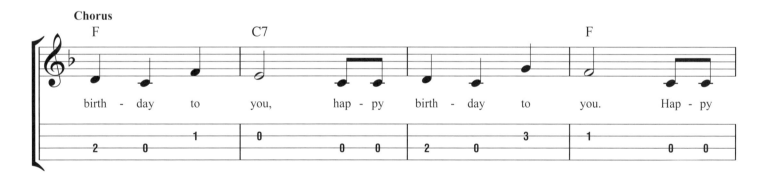

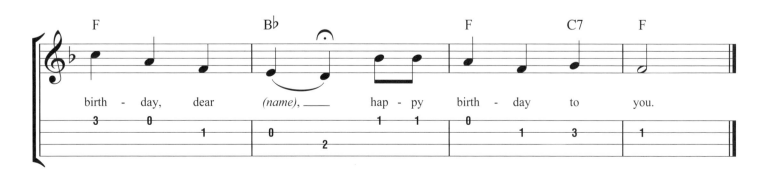

Fly Me to the Moon
(In Other Words)

Words and Music by Bart Howard

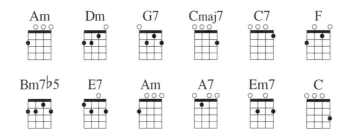

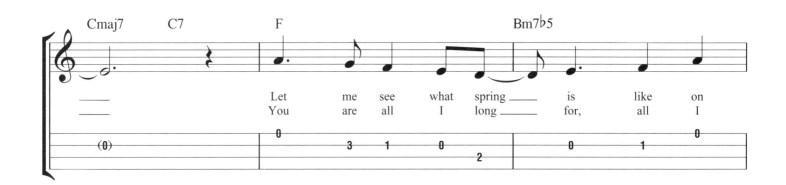

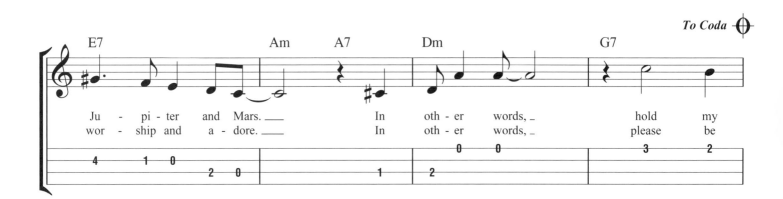

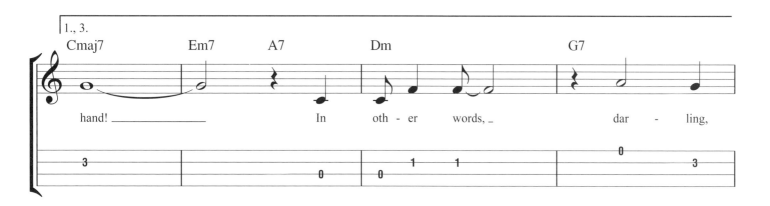

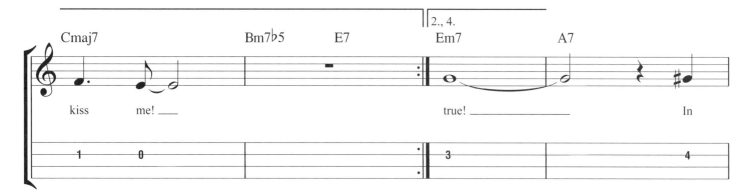

D.C. al Coda
(with repeat)

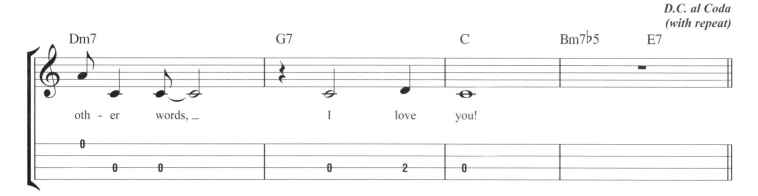

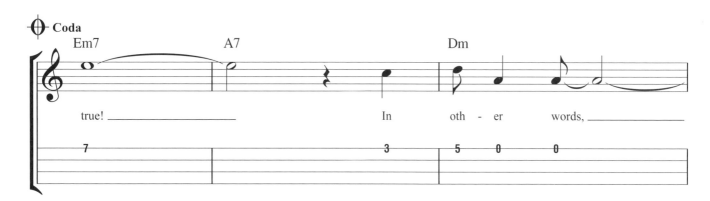

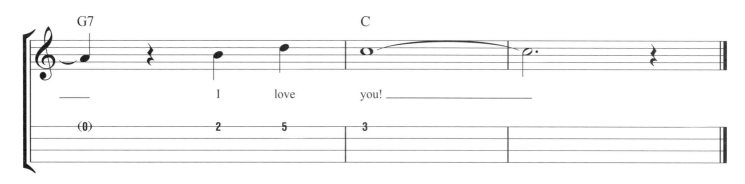

Goodnight, Irene

Words and Music by Huddie Ledbetter and John A. Lomax

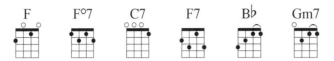

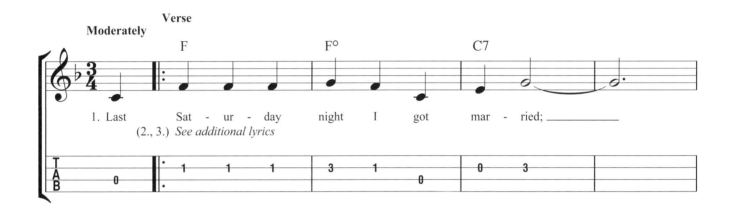

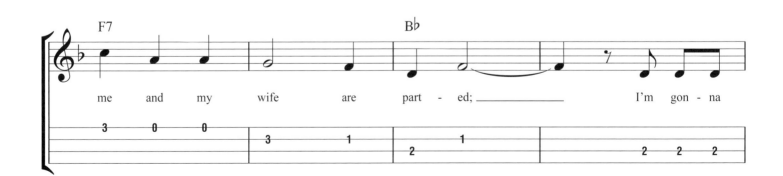

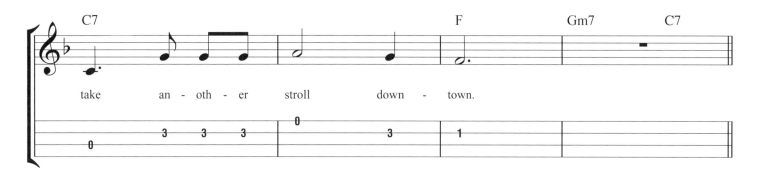

take an - oth - er stroll down - town.

Chorus

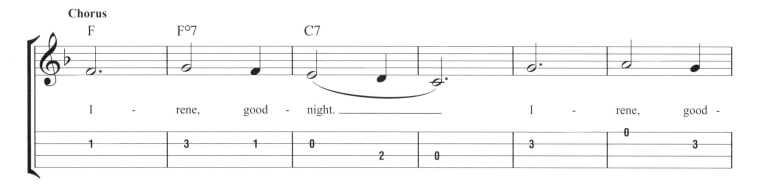

I - rene, good - night. _____ I - rene, good -

night. _____ Good - night, I - rene, good - night, I - rene; I'll

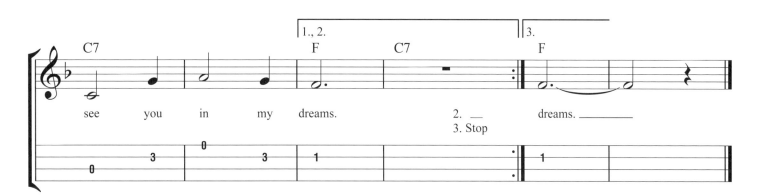

see you in my dreams.

1., 2.
2. __ dreams. _____
3. Stop

Additional Lyrics

2. Sometimes I live in the country,
Sometimes I live in the town.
Sometimes I have a great notion
To jump into the river and drown.

3. Stop ramblin', stop your gamblin',
Stop staying out late at night.
Go home to your wife and your fam'ly,
Sit down by the fireside bright.

Hallelujah

Words and Music by Leonard Cohen

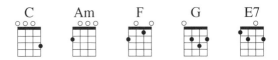

Verse
Moderately slow, in 2

1. I've heard there was a se-cret chord ____ that
(2.–5.) *See additional lyrics*

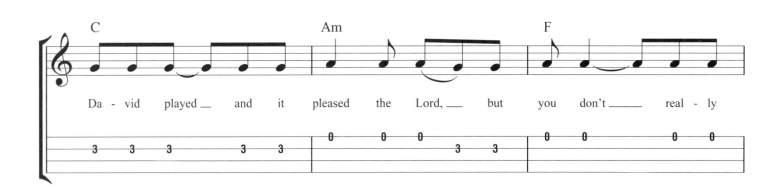

Da-vid played ___ and it pleased the Lord, ___ but you don't ___ real-ly

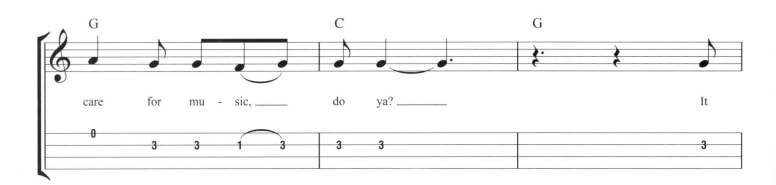

care for mu-sic, ____ do ya? _____ It

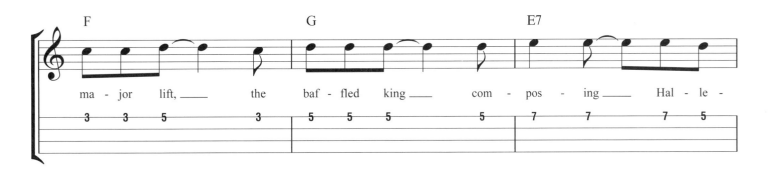

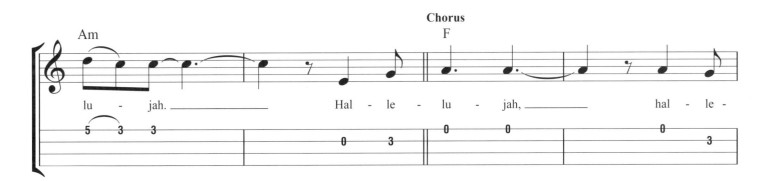

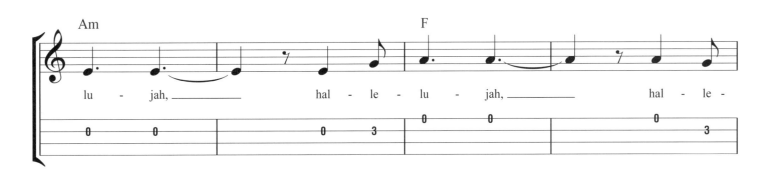

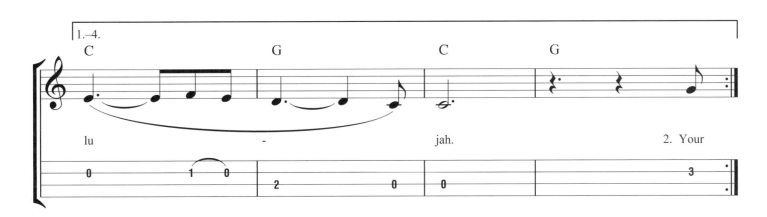

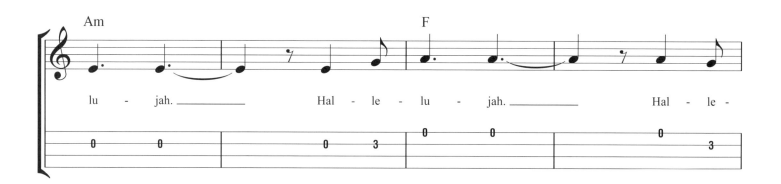

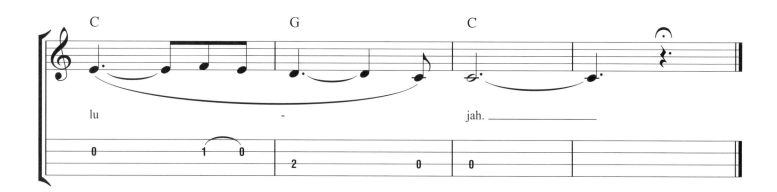

Additional Lyrics

2. Your faith was strong, but you needed proof.
   You saw her bathing on the roof.
   Her beauty and the moonlight overthrew ya.
   She tied you to a kitchen chair.
   She broke your throne, she cut your hair.
   And from your lips she drew the Hallelujah.

3. Maybe I have been here before.
   I know this room, I've walked this floor.
   I used to live alone before I knew ya.
   I've seen your flag on the marble arch.
   Love is not a vict'ry march.
   It's a cold and it's a broken Hallelujah.

4. There was a time you let me know
   What's real and going on below.
   But now you never show it to me, do ya?
   And remember when I moved in you.
   The holy dove was movin', too,
   And every breath we drew was Hallelujah.

5. Maybe there's a God above,
   And all I ever learned from love
   Was how to shoot at someone who outdrew ya.
   And it's not a cry you can hear at night.
   It's not somebody who's seen the light.
   It's a cold and it's a broken Hallelujah.

Kum Ba Yah

Traditional Spiritual

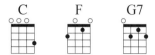

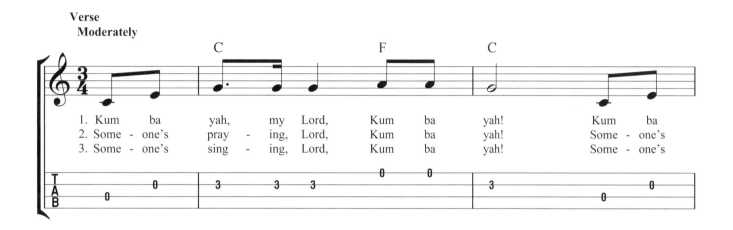

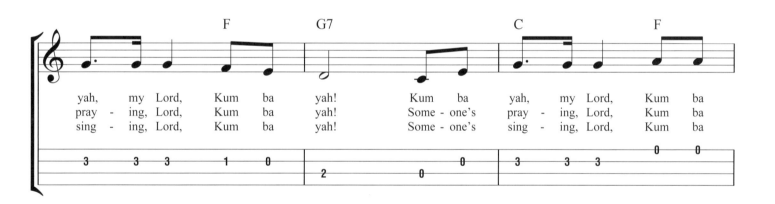

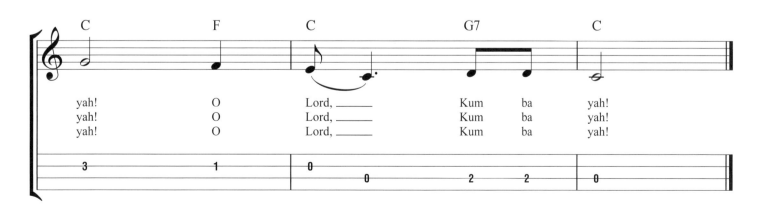

Heart and Soul

from the Paramount Short Subject A SONG IS BORN
Words by Frank Loesser
Music by Hoagy Carmichael

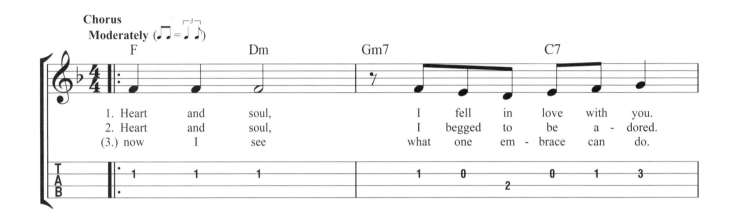

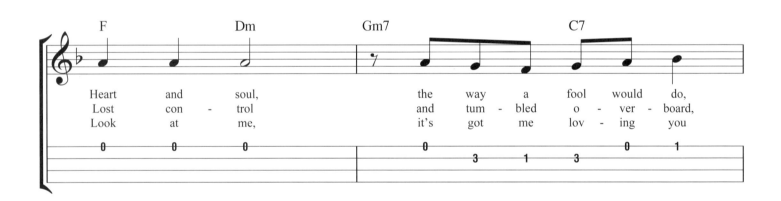

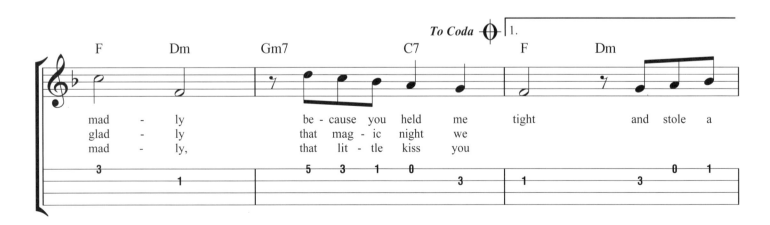

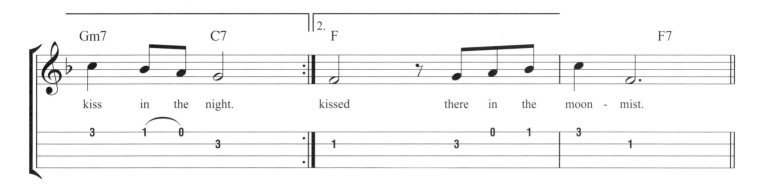

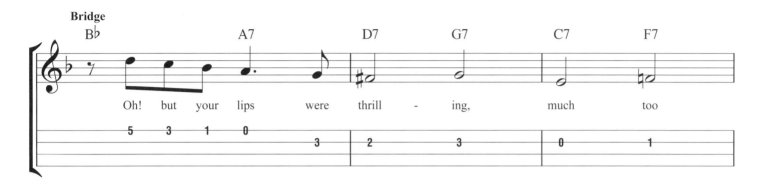

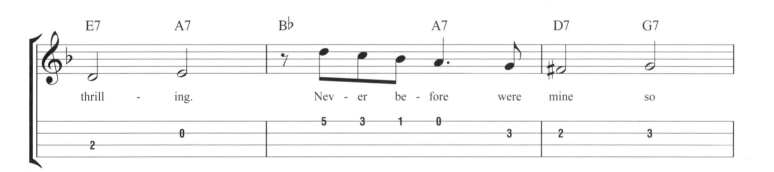

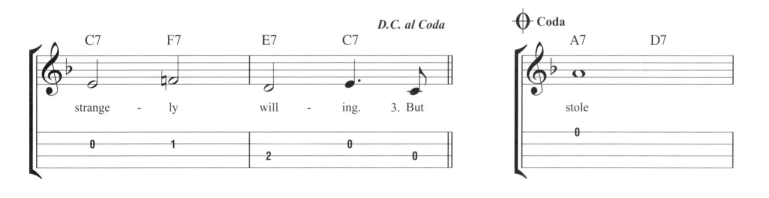

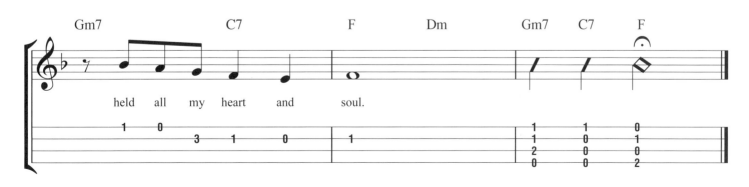

Home on the Range

Lyrics by Dr. Brewster Higley
Music by Dan Kelly

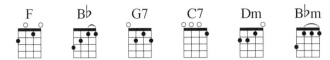

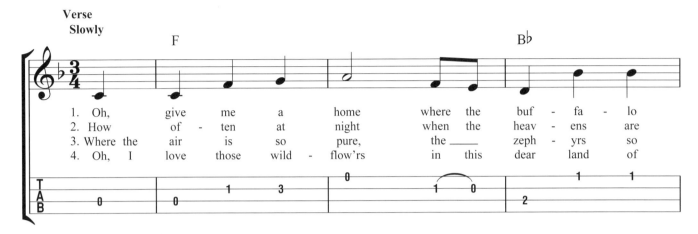

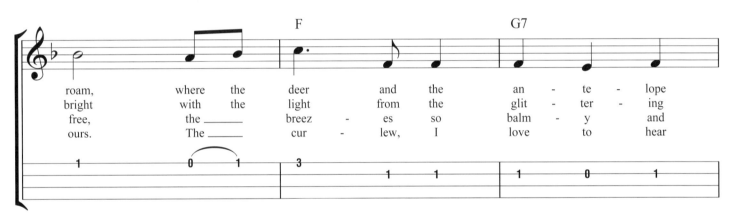

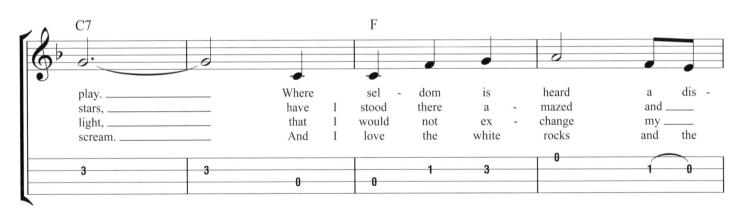

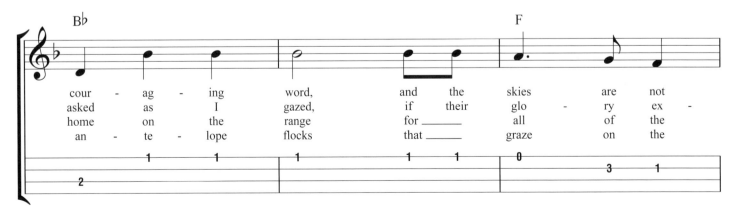

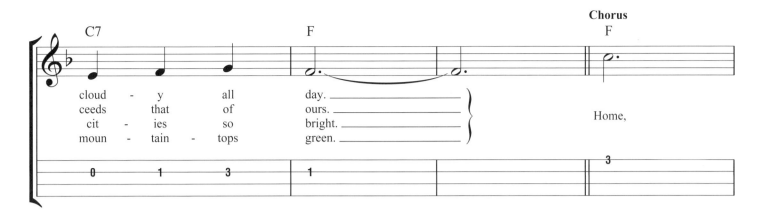

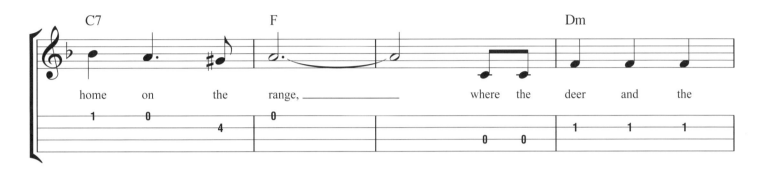

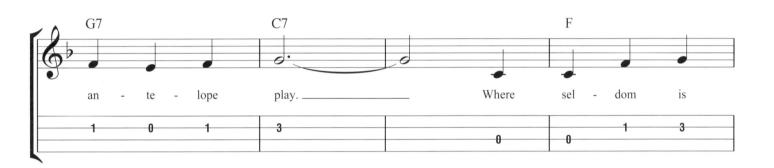

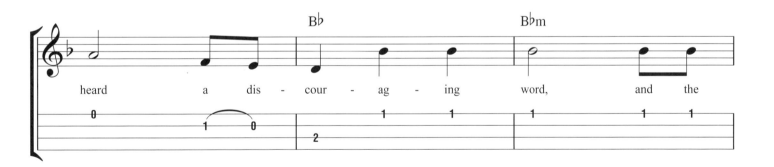

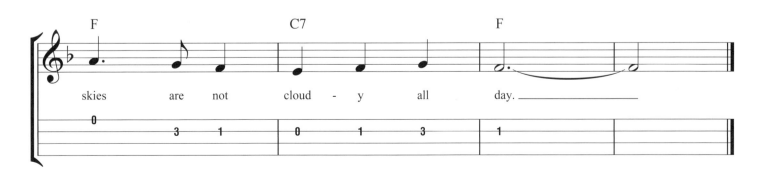

I Walk the Line

Words and Music by John R. Cash

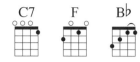

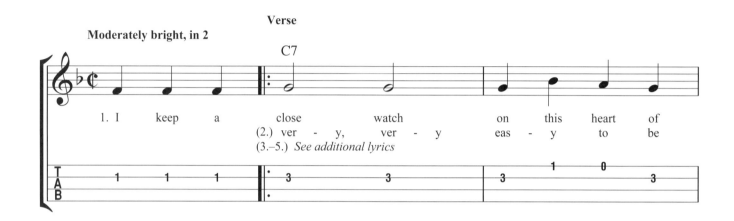

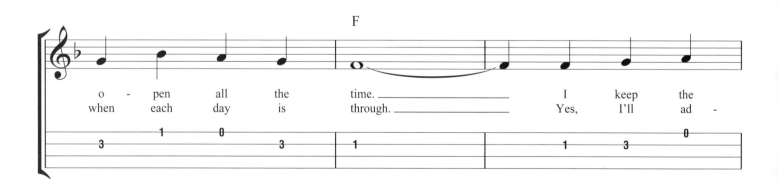

ends out that for the tie that binds. _____
mit that I'm a fool that for you. _____

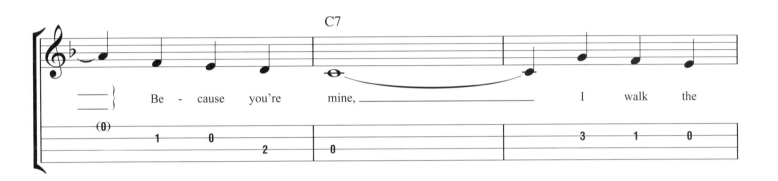

Be - cause you're mine, _____ I walk the

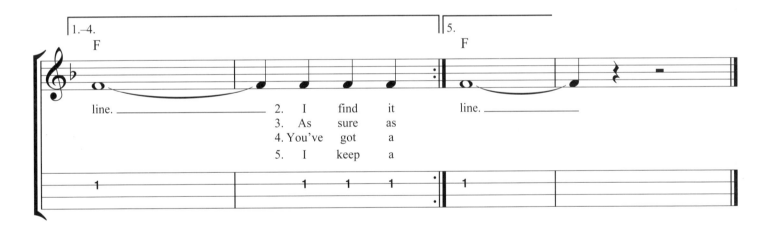

line. _____
        2. I find it
        3. As sure as
        4. You've got a
        5. I keep a

line. _____

Additional Lyrics

3. As sure as night is dark and day is light,
   I keep you on my mind both day and night.
   And happiness I've known proves that it's right.
   Because you're mine, I walk the line.

4. You've got a way to keep me on your side.
   You give me a cause for love that I can't hide.
   For you I know I'd even try to turn the tide.
   Because you're mine, I walk the line.

5. I keep a close watch on this heart of mine.
   I keep my eyes wide open all the time.
   I keep the ends out for the tie that binds.
   Because you're mine, I walk the line.

I'd Like to Teach the World to Sing

Words and Music by Bill Backer, Roquel Davis, Roger Cook and Roger Greenaway

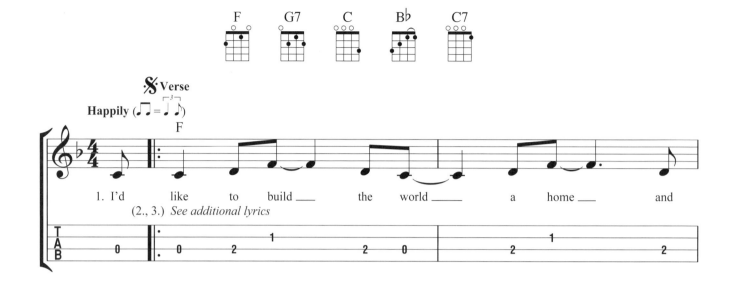

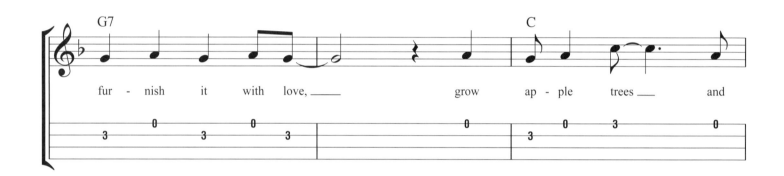

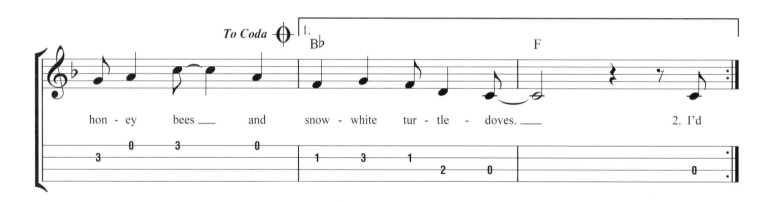

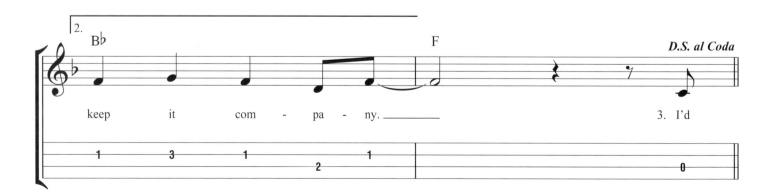

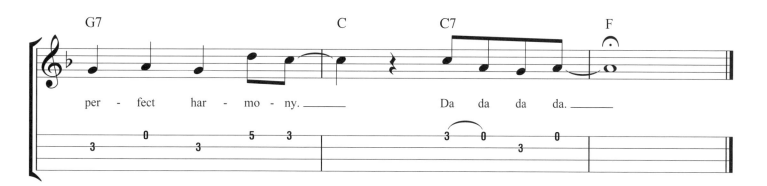

Additional Lyrics

2. I'd like to teach the world to sing in perfect harmony.
   I'd like to hold it in my arms and keep it company.

3. I'd like to see the world, for once, all standing hand in hand,
   And hear them echo through the hills for peace throughout the land.

I'm So Lonesome I Could Cry

Words and Music by Hank Williams

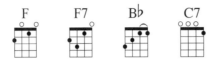

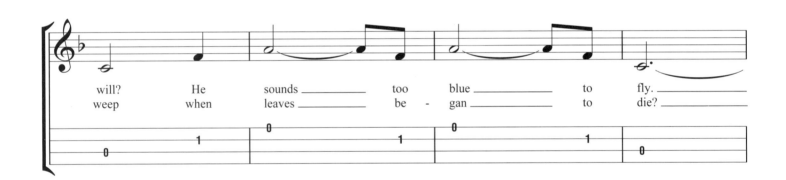

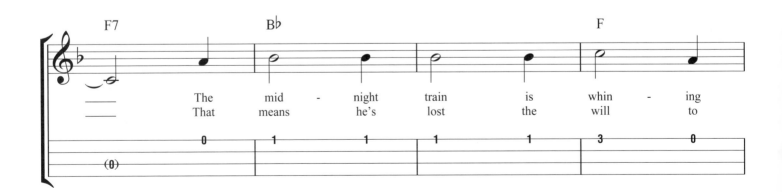

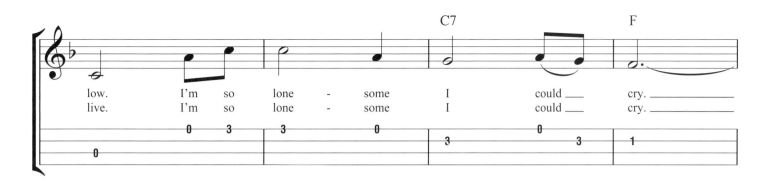

low.   I'm so lone - some I could   cry.
live.   I'm so lone - some I could   cry.

Verse

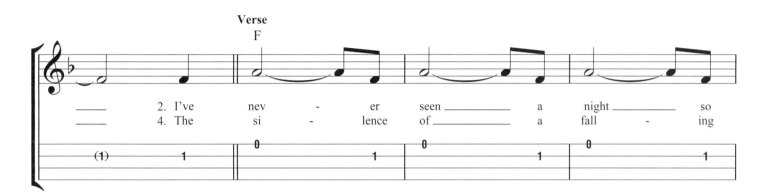

2. I've nev - er seen _____ a night _____ so
4. The si - lence of _____ a fall - ing

long when time _____ goes crawl - ing by. _____ The
star lights up _____ a pur - ple sky. _____ And

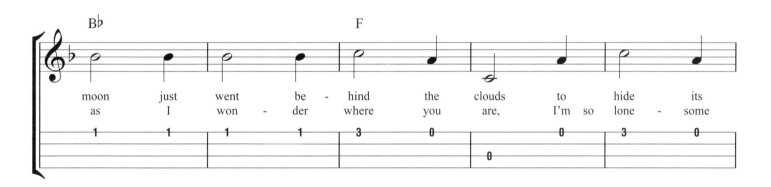

moon just went be - hind the clouds to hide its
as I won - der where you are, I'm so lone - some

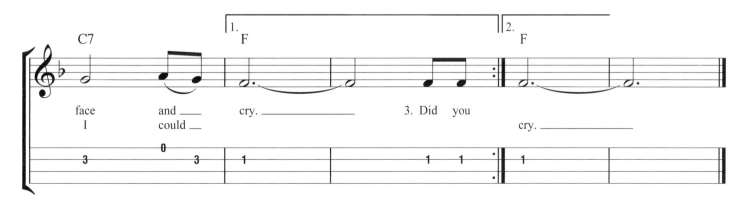

face and ___ cry. _____ 3. Did you
I could ___ cry. _____

Last Night I Had the Strangest Dream

Words and Music by Ed McCurdy

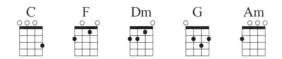

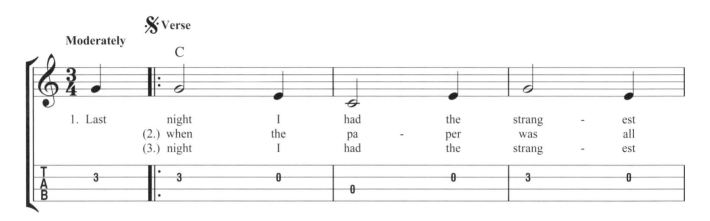

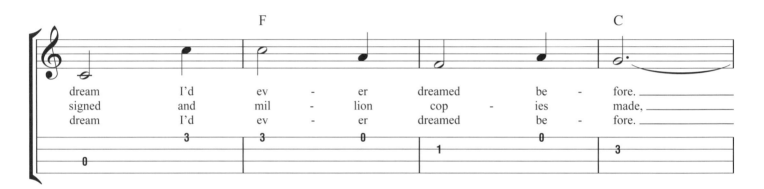

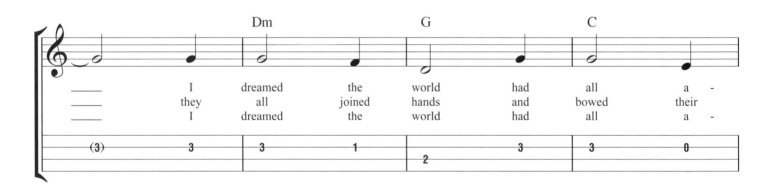

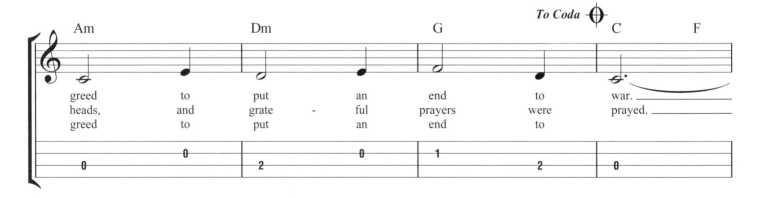

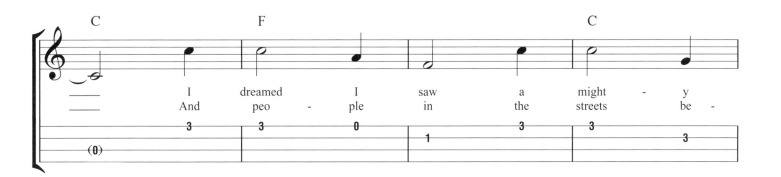

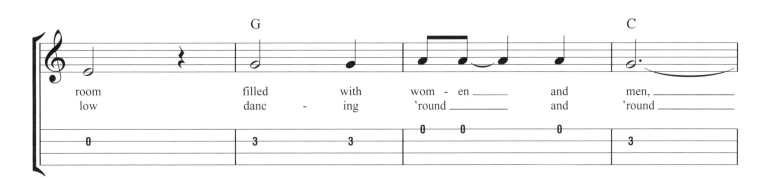

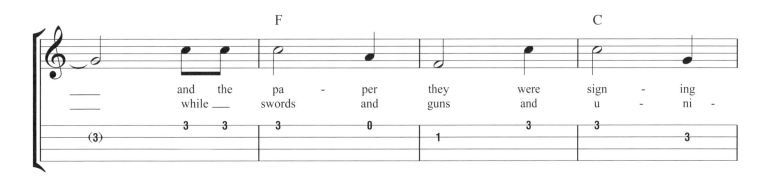

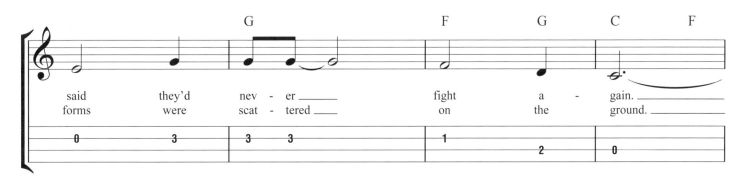

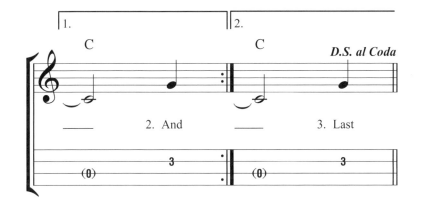

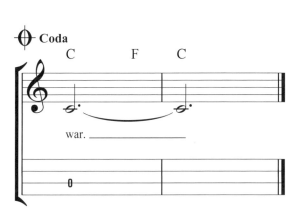

Love Me Tender

Words and Music by Elvis Presley and Vera Matson

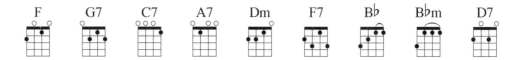

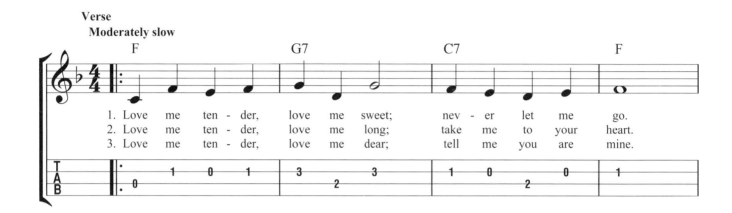

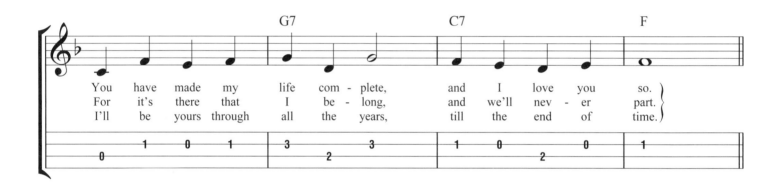

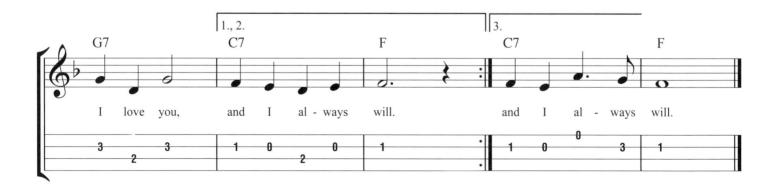

Mr. Tambourine Man

Words and Music by Bob Dylan

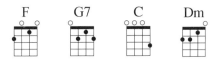

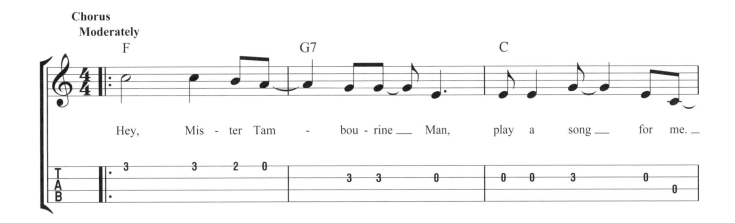

Hey, Mis - ter Tam - bou - rine Man, play a song for me.

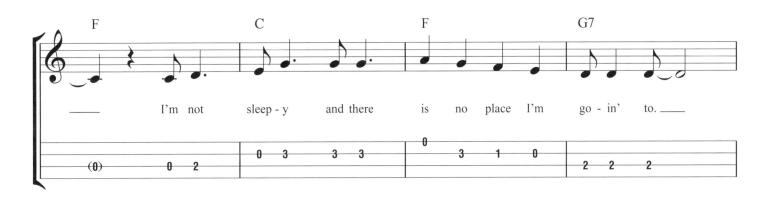

I'm not sleep - y and there is no place I'm go - in' to.

Hey, Mis - ter Tam - bou - rine Man, play a song for me.

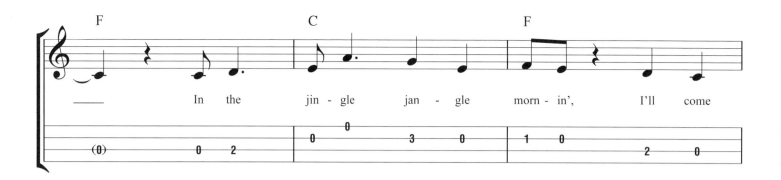

In the jin - gle jan - gle morn - in', I'll come

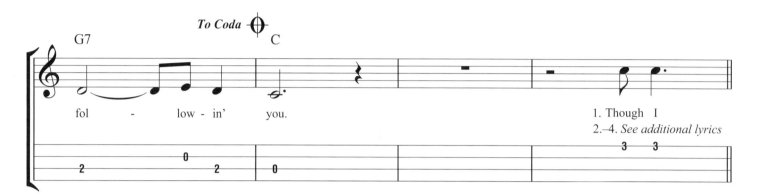

To Coda ⊕

fol - low - in' you.

1. Though I
2.–4. *See additional lyrics*

Verse

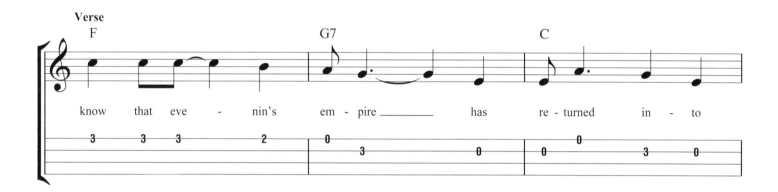

know that eve - nin's em - pire ___ has re - turned in - to

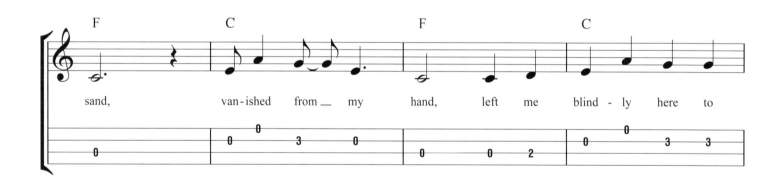

sand, van - ished from ___ my hand, left me blind - ly here to

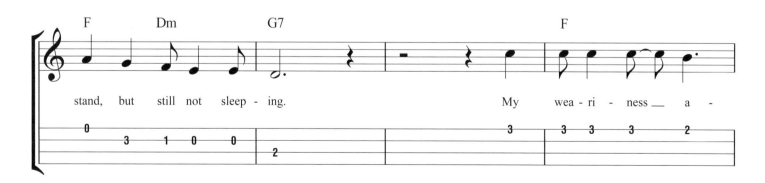

stand, but still not sleep - ing. My wea - ri - ness ___ a -

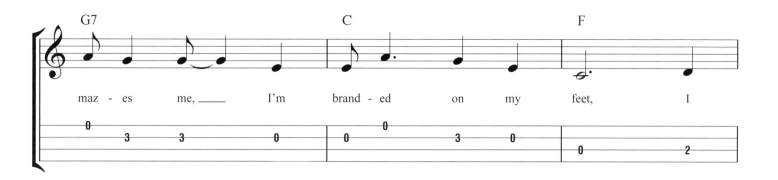

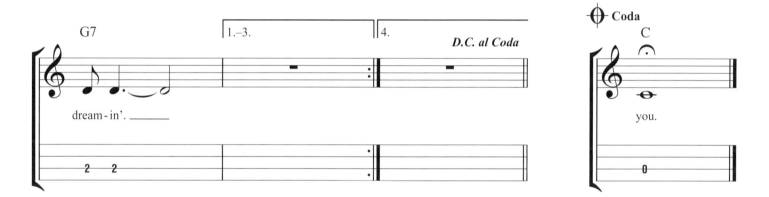

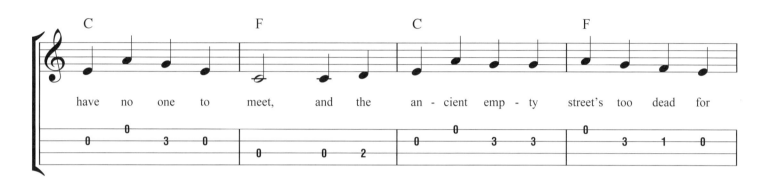

Additional Lyrics

2. Take me on a trip upon your magic swirlin' ship.
   My senses have been stripped, my hands can't feel to grip.
   My toes too numb to step, wait only for my boot heels to be wanderin'.
   I'm ready to go anywhere, I'm ready for to fade
   Into my own parade, cast your dancin' spell my way.
   I promise to go under it.

3. Though you might hear laughin', spinnin', swingin' madly across the sun,
   It's not aimed at anyone, it's just escapin' on the run.
   And but for the sky, there are no fences facin',
   And if you hear vague traces of skippin' reels of rhyme
   To your tambourine in time, it's just a ragged clown behind.
   I wouldn't pay it any mind; it's just a shadow you're seein' that he's chasin'.

4. Then take me disappearin' through the smoke rings of my mind,
   Down the foggy ruins of time, far past the frozen leaves,
   The haunted, frightened trees out to the windy beach,
   Far from the twisted reach of crazy sorrow,
   Yes, to dance beneath the diamond sky with one hand wavin' free,
   Silhouetted by the sea, circled by the circus sands,
   With all memory and fate driven deep beneath the waves.

Mack the Knife

from THE THREEPENNY OPERA

English Words by Marc Blitzstein
Original German Words by Bert Brecht
Music by Kurt Weill

Verse

Moderately, in 2

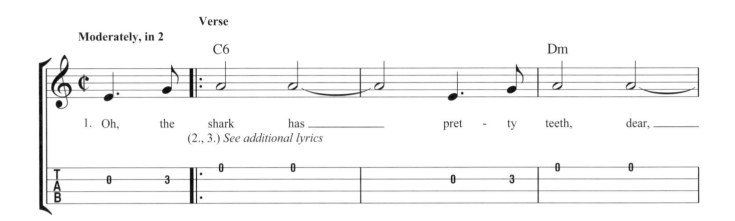

1. Oh, the shark has _____ pret - ty teeth, dear, _____
(2., 3.) *See additional lyrics*

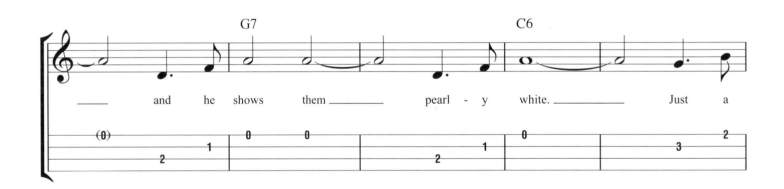

___ and he shows them _____ pearl - y white. _____ Just a

jack - knife _____ has Mac - heath, dear, _____ and he keeps it _____

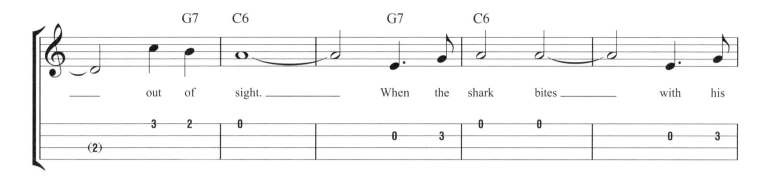

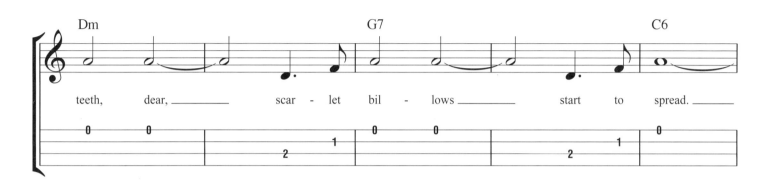

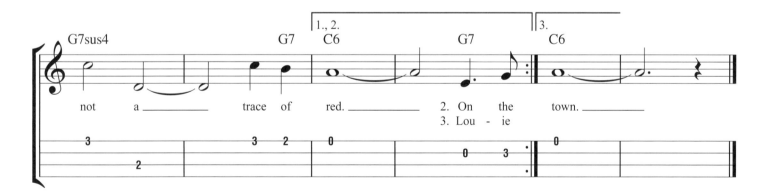

Additional Lyrics

2. On the sidewalk Sunday morning lies a body oozing life.
Someone's sneaking 'round the corner; is the someone Mack the Knife?
From a tugboat by the river, a cement bag's dropping down.
The cement's just for the weight, dear; bet you Mackie's back in town.

3. Louie Miller disappeared, dear, after drawing out his cash.
And Macheath spends like a sailor; did our boy do something rash?
Sukey Tawdry, Jenny Diver, Polly Peachum, Lucy Brown.
Oh, the line forms on the right, dear, now that Mackie's back in town.

Moon River

from the Paramount Picture BREAKFAST AT TIFFANY'S
Words by Johnny Mercer
Music by Henry Mancini

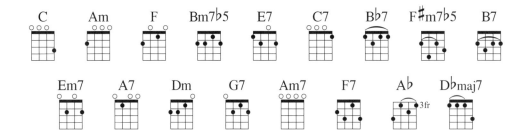

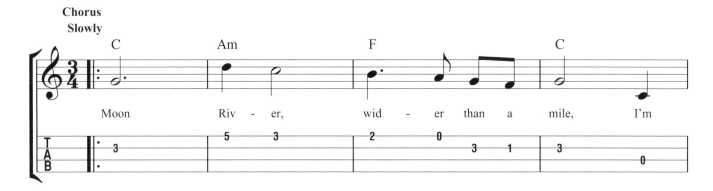

Chorus
Slowly

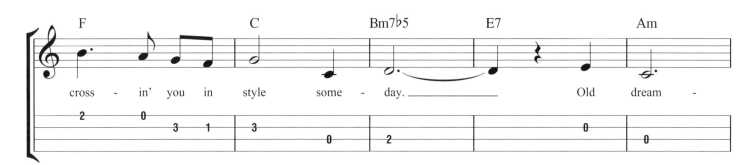

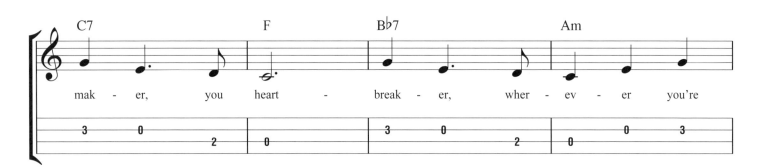

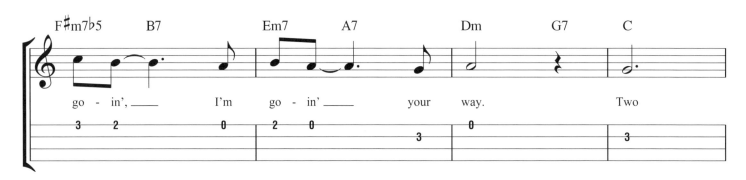

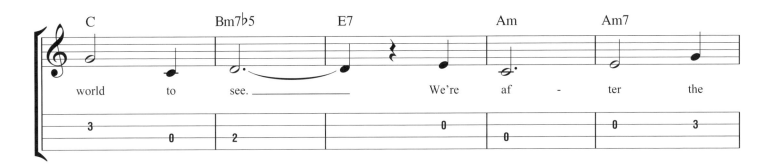

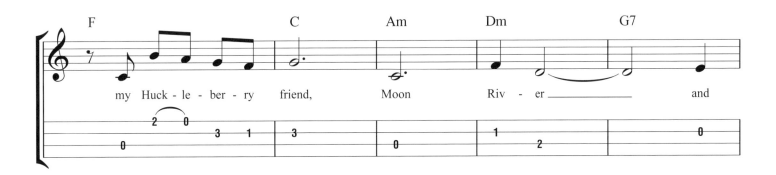

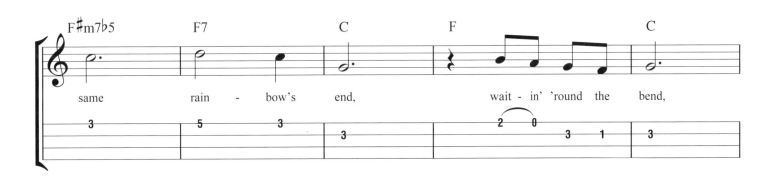

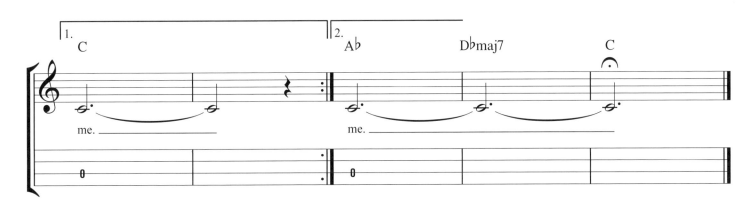

Morning Has Broken

Words by Eleanor Farjeon
Music by Cat Stevens

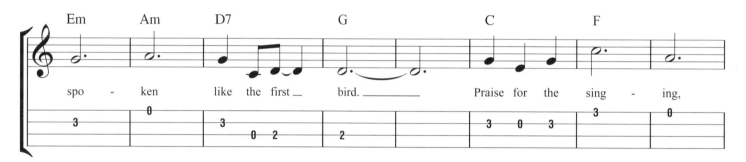

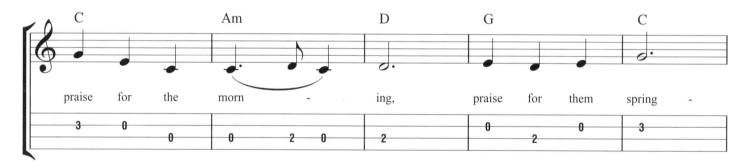

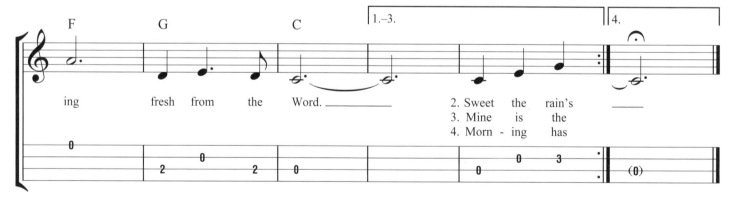

Additional Lyrics

2. Sweet the rain's new fall, sunlit from heaven,
   Like the first dewfall on the first grass.
   Praise for the sweetness of the wet garden,
   Sprung in completeness where His feet pass.

3. Mine is the sunlight, mine is the morning,
   Born of the one light Eden saw play.
   Praise with elation, praise ev'ry morning,
   God's recreation of the new day.

Puff the Magic Dragon

Words and Music by Lenny Lipton and Peter Yarrow

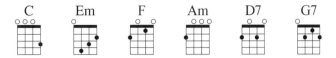

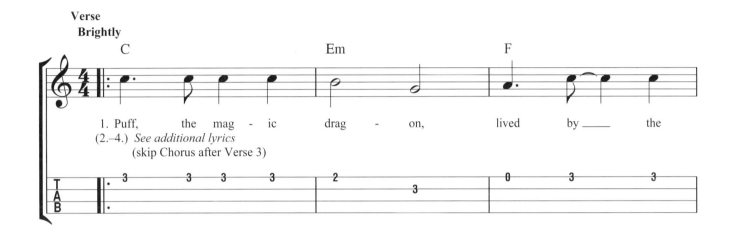

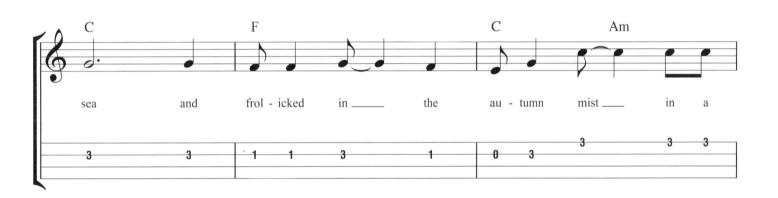

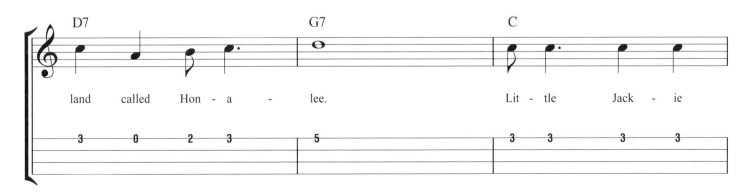

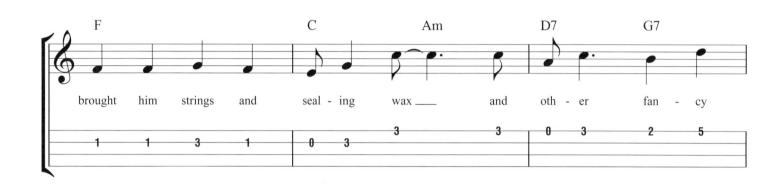

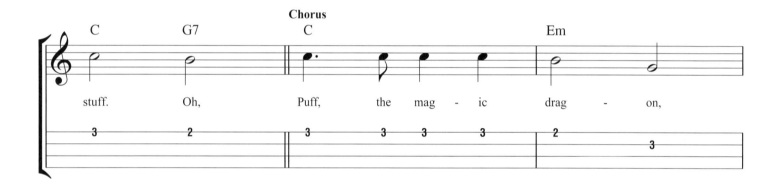

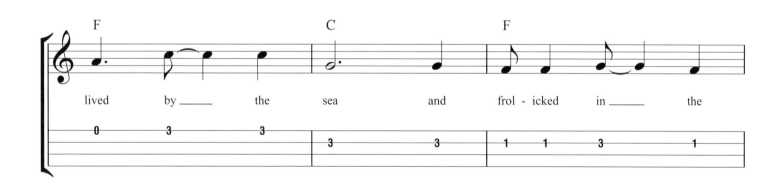

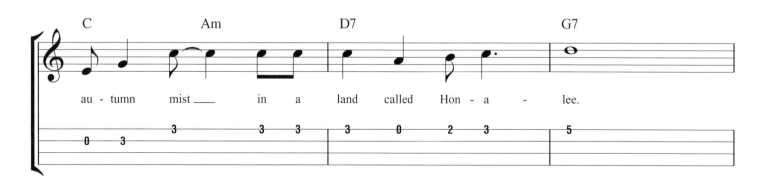

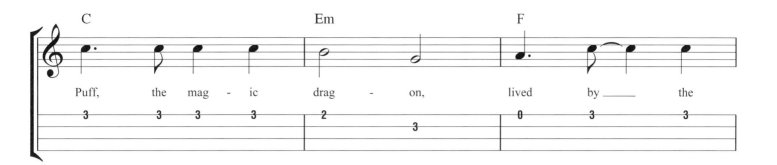

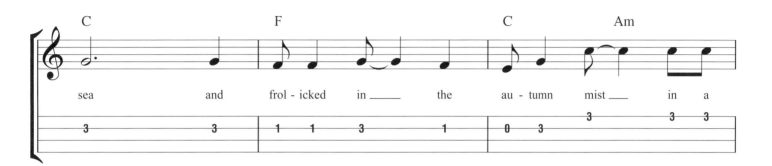

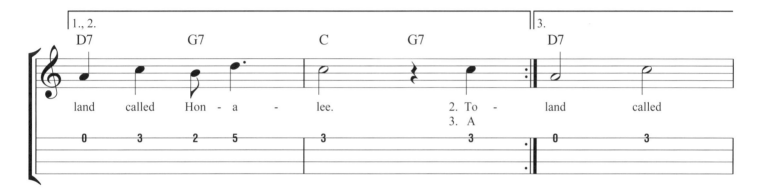

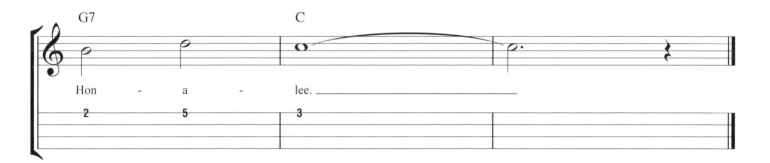

Additional Lyrics

2. Together they would travel on a boat with billowed sail,
   And Jackie kept a lookout perched on Puff's gigantic tail.
   Noble kings and princes would bow whenever they came.
   Pirate ships would lower their flags when Puff roared out his name.

3. A dragon lives forever, but not so little boys.
   Painted wings and giant rings make way for other toys.
   One gray night it happened; Jackie Paper came no more,
   And Puff, that mighty dragon, he ceased his fearless roar. *(To Verse 4)*

4. His head was bent in sorrow, green tears fell like rain.
   Puff no longer went to play along the Cherry Lane.
   Without his lifelong friend, Puff could not be brave.
   So Puff, that mighty dragon, sadly slipped into his cave.

My Heart Will Go On
(Love Theme from 'Titanic')

from the Paramount and Twentieth Century Fox Motion Picture TITANIC

Music by James Horner
Lyric by Will Jennings

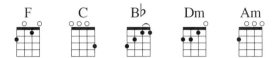

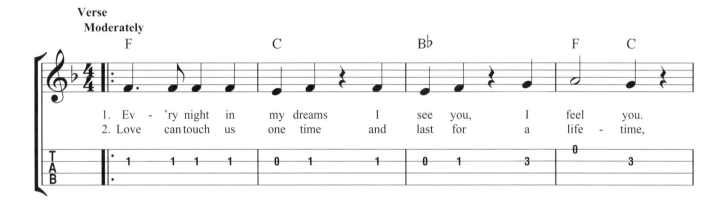

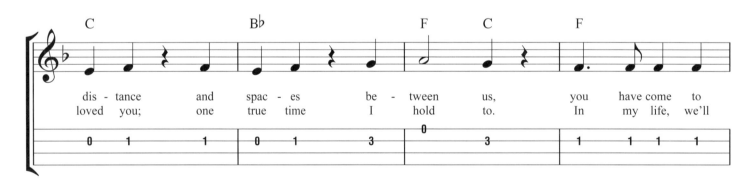

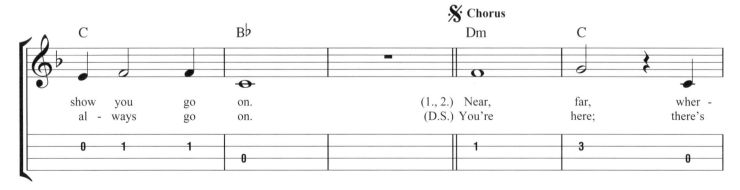

ev - er you are, _____ I be - lieve that the heart does go
noth - ing I fear, _____ and I know that my heart will go

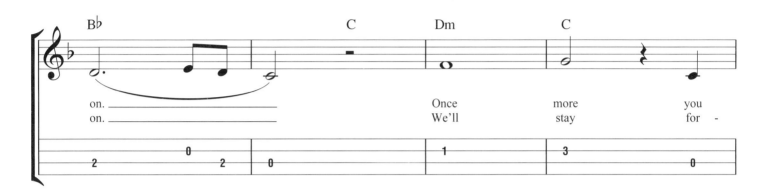

on. _____
on. _____ Once more you
We'll more stay you for -

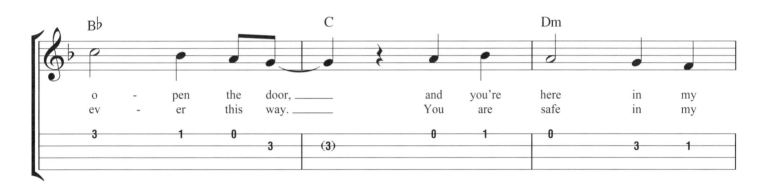

o - pen the door, _____ and you're here in my
ev - er this way. _____ You are here safe in my

To Coda ⊕

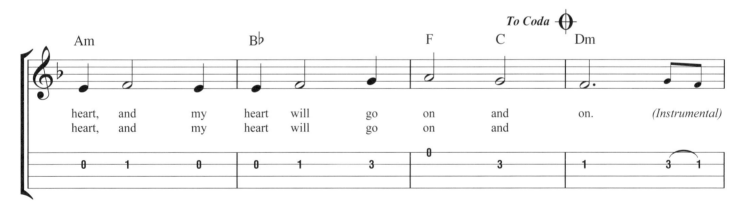

heart, and my heart will go on and on. *(Instrumental)*
heart, and my heart will go on and

2nd time, D.S. al Coda ⊕ **Coda**

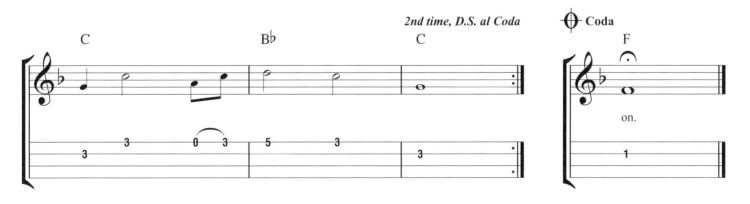

on.

Norwegian Wood
(This Bird Has Flown)

Words and Music by John Lennon and Paul McCartney

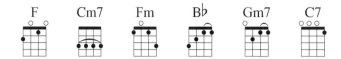

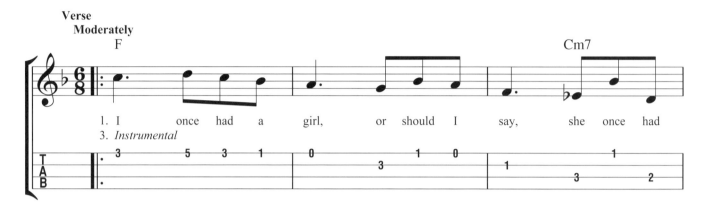

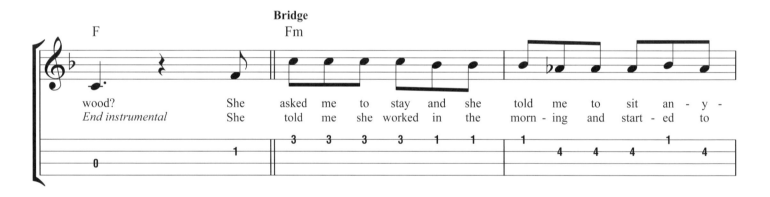

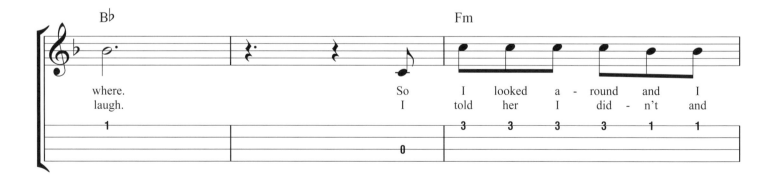

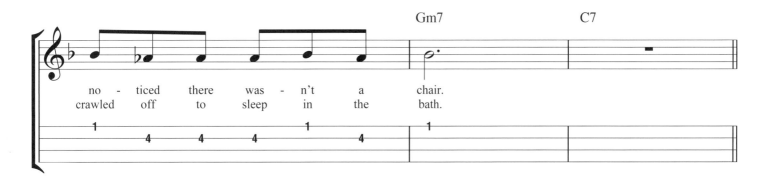

no - ticed there was - n't a chair.
crawled off to sleep in the bath.

Verse

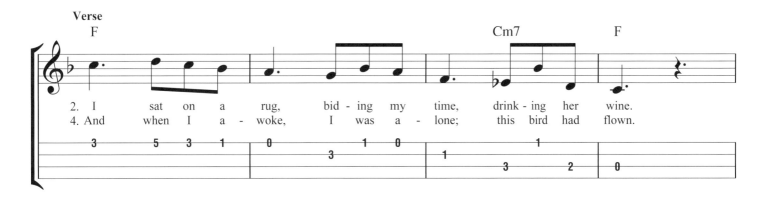

2. I sat on a rug, bid - ing my time, drink - ing her wine.
4. And when I a - woke, I was a - lone; this bird had flown.

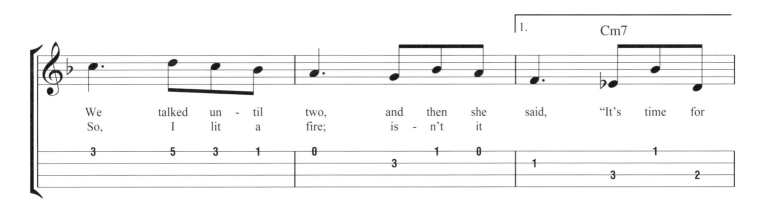

We talked un - til two, and then she said, "It's time for
So, I lit a fire; is - n't it

bed." good Nor - we - gian wood?

Outro

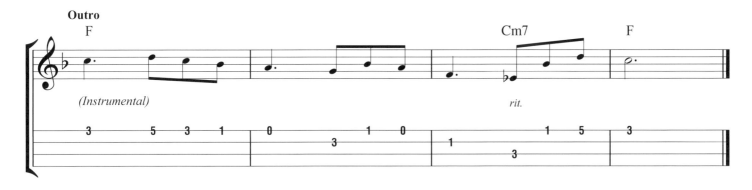

(Instrumental) *rit.*

Rock Around the Clock

Words and Music by Max C. Freedman and Jimmy DeKnight

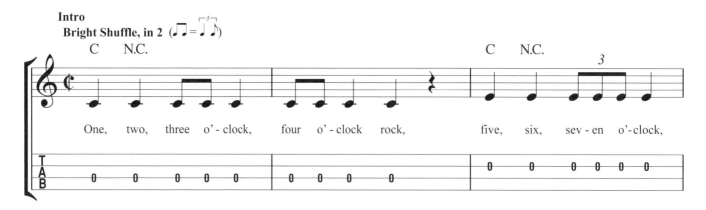

Intro
Bright Shuffle, in 2

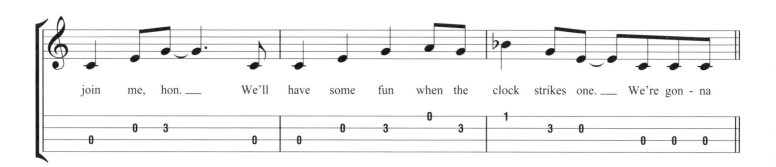

Chorus

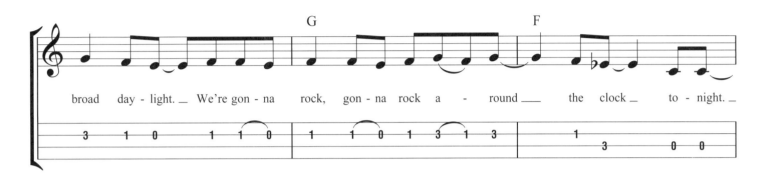

rock   a - round   the   clock   to - night, __   we're gon - na   rock,   rock,   rock   'til

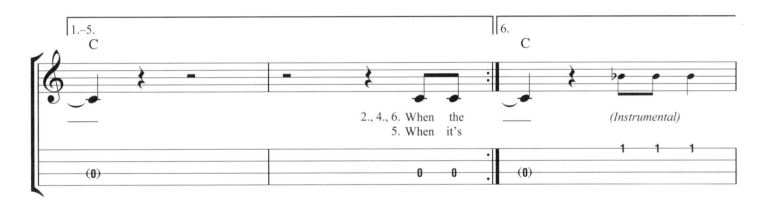

broad   day - light. __   We're gon - na   rock,   gon - na rock a -   round ___   the   clock __   to - night. __

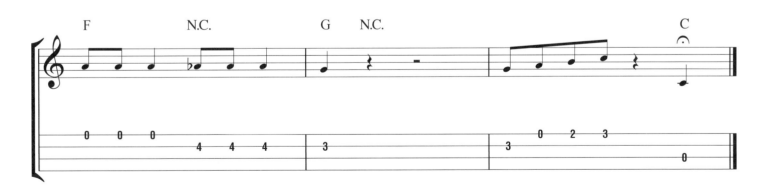

2., 4., 6. When   the ___
5. When   it's

(Instrumental)

Additional Lyrics

2. When the clock strikes two, and three and four,
   If the band slows down, we'll yell for more.

4. When the chimes ring five and six and seven,
   We'll be rockin' up in seventh heav'n.

5. When it's eight, nine, ten, eleven, too,
   I'll be goin' strong and so will you.

6. When the clock strikes twelve, we'll cool off, then,
   Start a rockin' 'round the clock again.

Rocky Top

Words and Music by Boudleaux Bryant and Felice Bryant

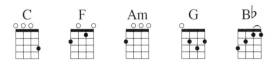

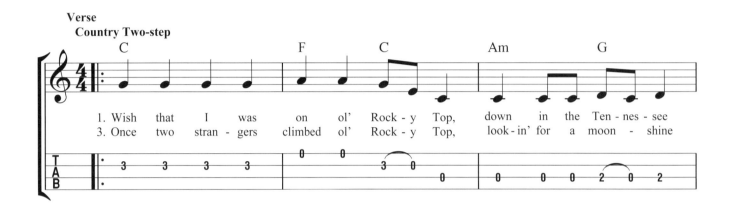

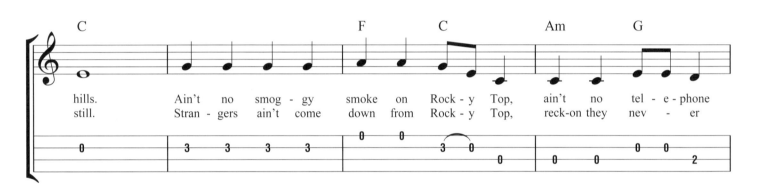

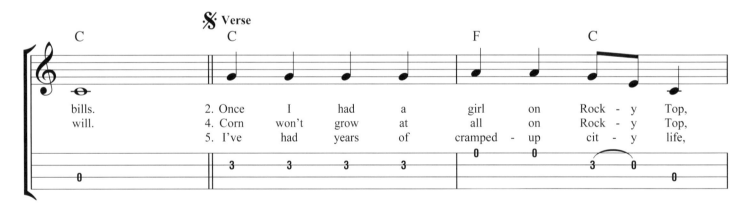

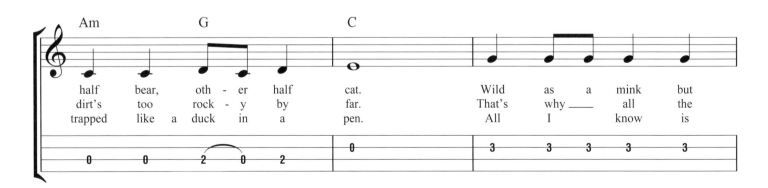

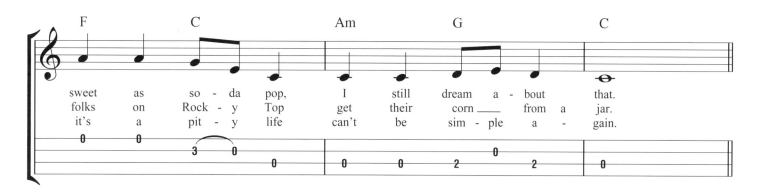

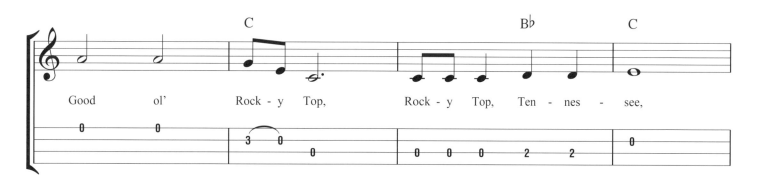

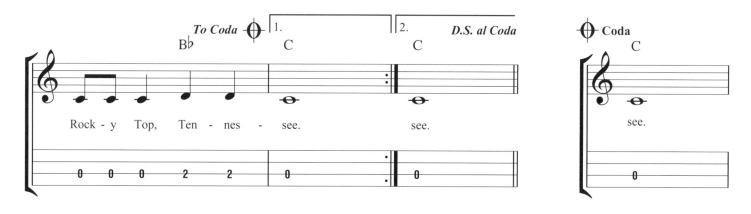

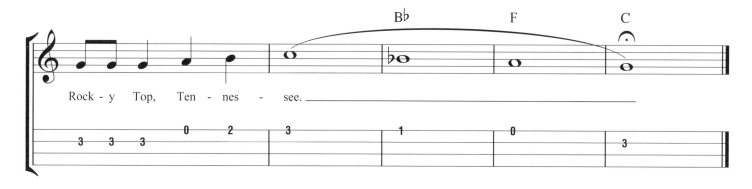

Simple Gifts

Traditional Shaker Hymn

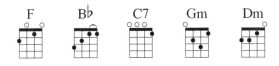

The Streets of Laredo

American Cowboy Song

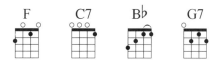

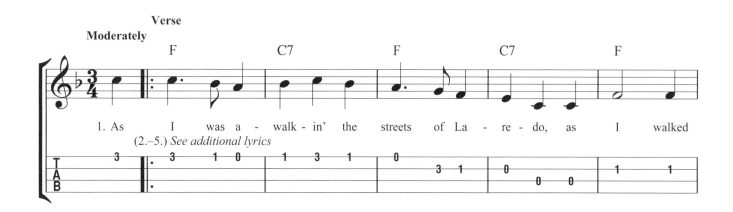

Verse

Moderately

1. As I was a-walk-in' the streets of La-re-do, as I walked
(2.–5.) *See additional lyrics*

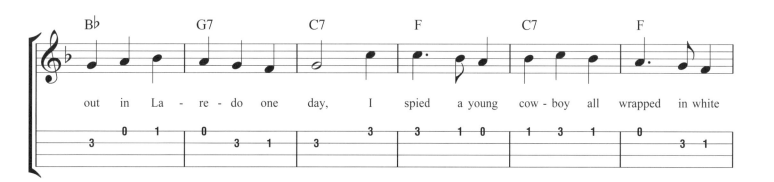

out in La-re-do one day, I spied a young cow-boy all wrapped in white

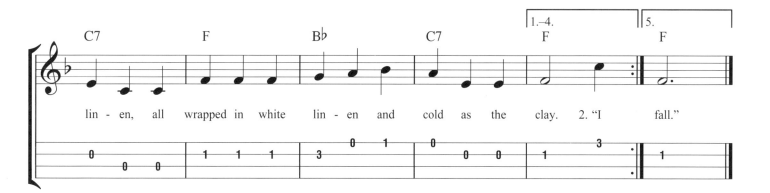

lin-en, all wrapped in white lin-en and cold as the clay. 2. "I fall."

Additional Lyrics

2. "I see by your outfit that you are a cowboy,"
These words he did say as I boldly walked by.
"Come sit down beside me and hear my sad story.
I'm shot in the breast and I know I must die."

3. "It was once in the saddle I used to go dashing,
Once in the saddle I used to go gay.
First down to Rosie's and then to the card house.
Got shot in the breast and I'm dying today."

4. "Get sixteen gamblers to carry my coffin,
Let six jolly cowboys come sing me a song.
Take me to the graveyard and lay the sod o'er me,
For I'm a young cowboy and I know I've done wrong."

5. "Oh, bang the drum slowly and play the fife lowly,
Play the dead march as you carry me along.
Put bunches of roses all over my coffin,
Roses to deaden the clods as they fall."

Strangers in the Night

adapted from A MAN COULD GET KILLED
Words by Charles Singleton and Eddie Snyder
Music by Bert Kaempfert

Verse
Moderately slow

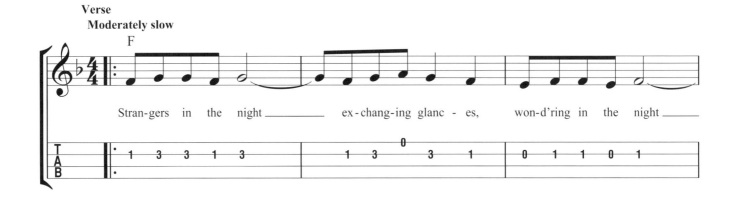

Stran-gers in the night _____ ex-chang-ing glanc - es, won-d'ring in the night _____

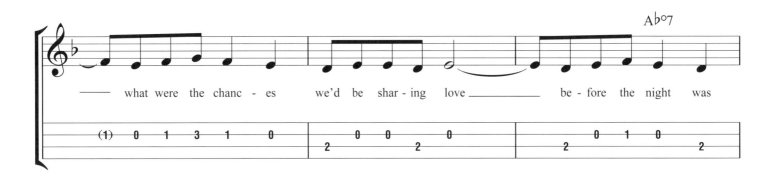

_____ what were the chanc - es we'd be shar - ing love _____ be - fore the night was

through. _____ Some-thing in your eyes _____ was so in - vit - ing.

Some-thing in your smile _____ was so ex - cit - ing. Some-thing in my heart _____

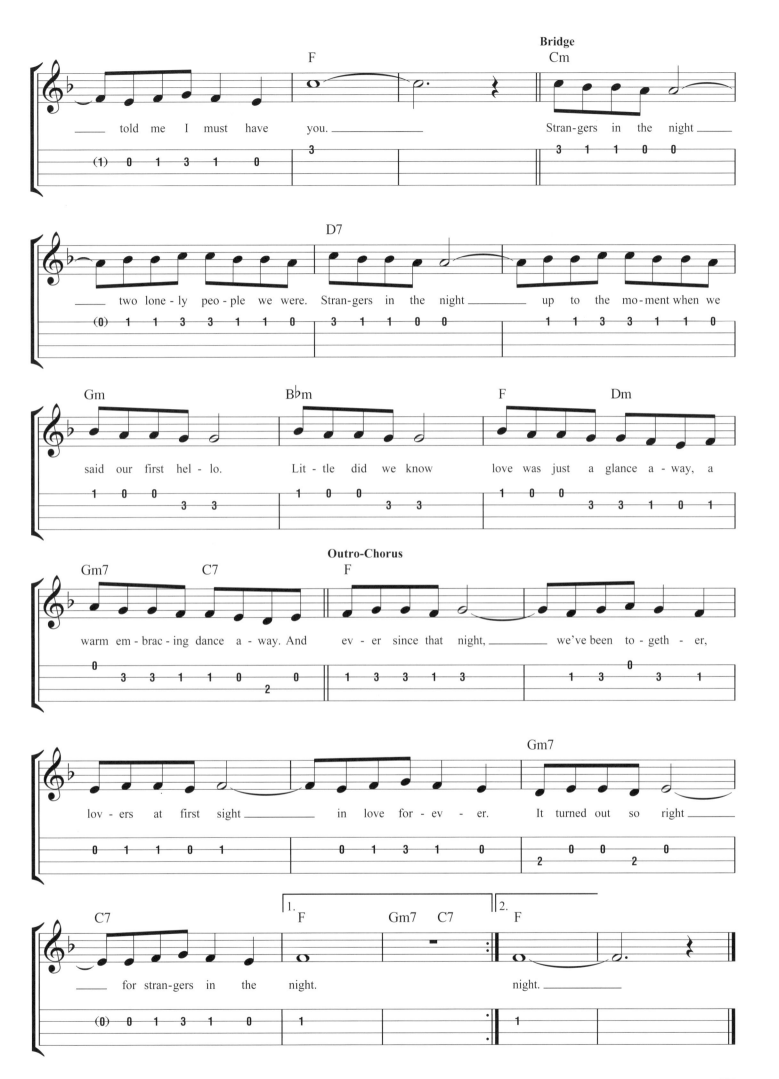

Tears in Heaven

Words and Music by Eric Clapton and Will Jennings

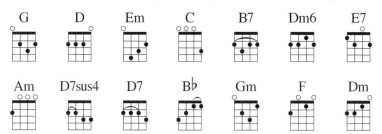

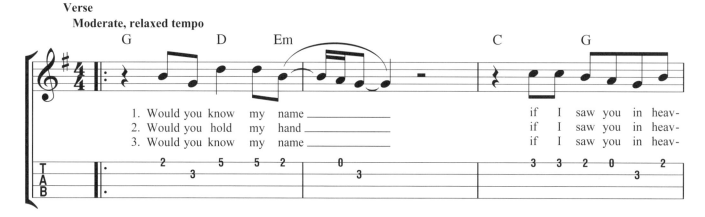

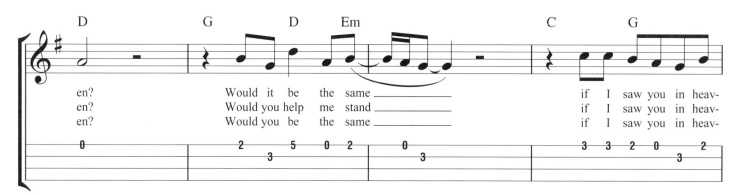

This Land Is Your Land

Words and Music by Woody Guthrie

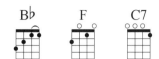

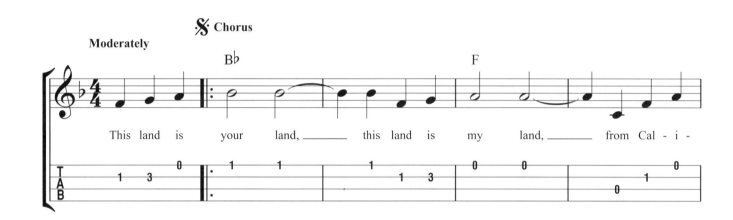

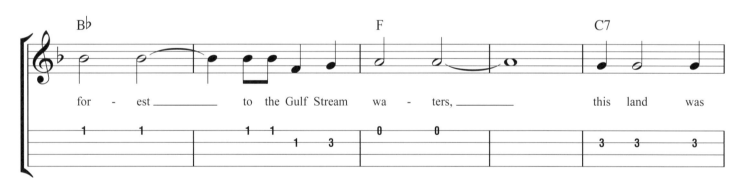

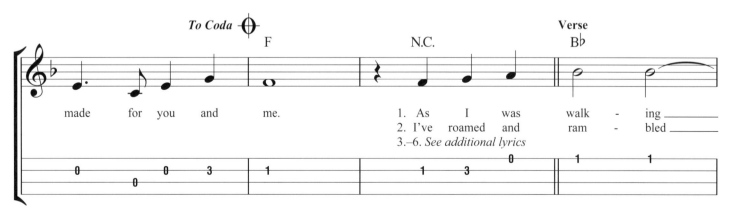

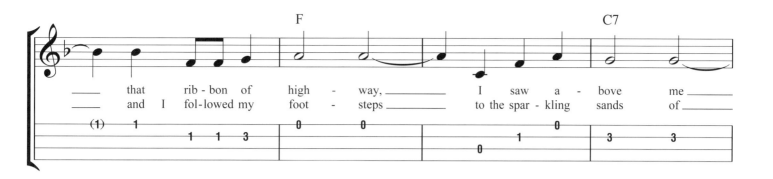

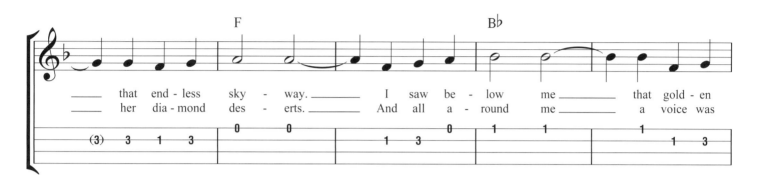

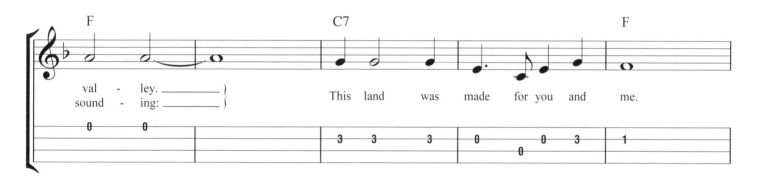

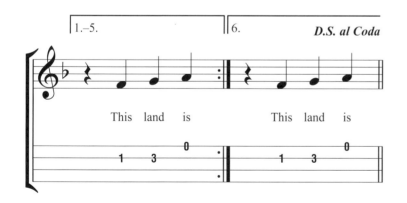

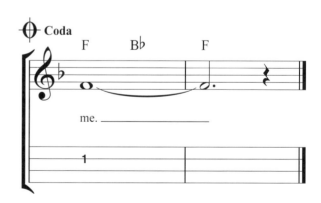

Additional Lyrics

3. When the sun came shining, and I was strolling,
   And the wheat fields waving, and the dust clouds rolling,
   As the fog was lifting, a voice was chanting:
   This land was made for you and me.

4. As I went walking, I saw a sign there,
   And on the sign it said, "No Trespassing,"
   But on the other side it didn't say nothing;
   That side was made for you and me.

5. In the shadow of the steeple, I saw my people.
   By the relief office, I saw my people.
   As they stood there hungry, I stood there asking:
   Is this land made for you and me?

6. Nobody living can ever stop me
   As I go walking that freedom highway.
   Nobody living can ever make me turn back;
   This land was made for you and me.

Time After Time

Words and Music by Cyndi Lauper and Rob Hyman

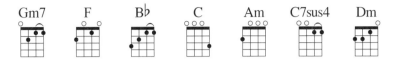

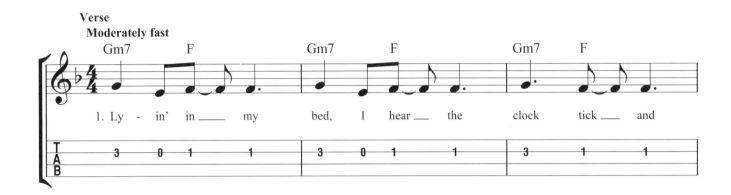

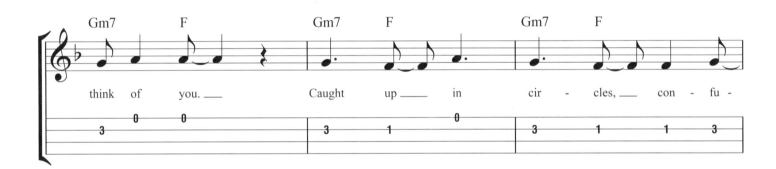

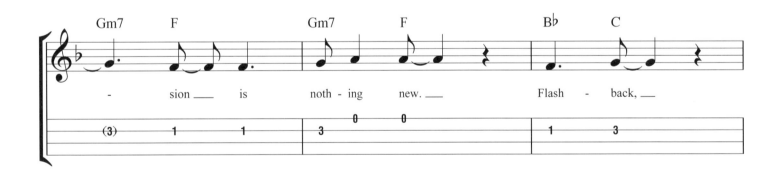

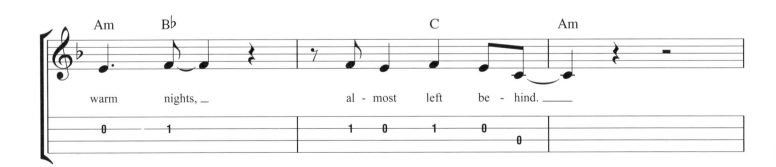

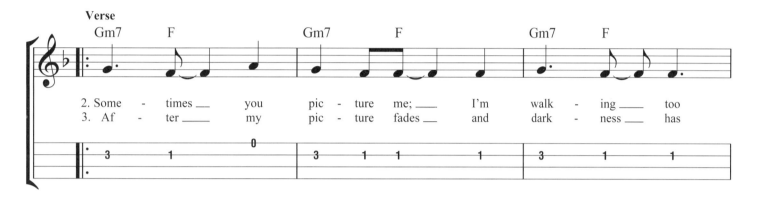

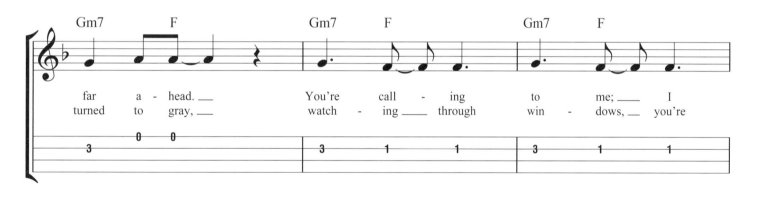

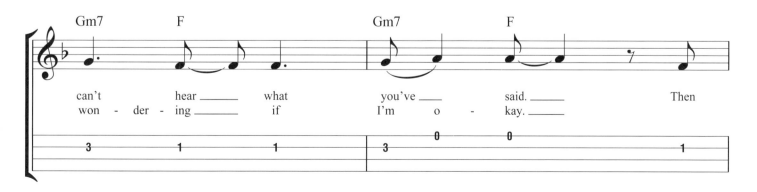

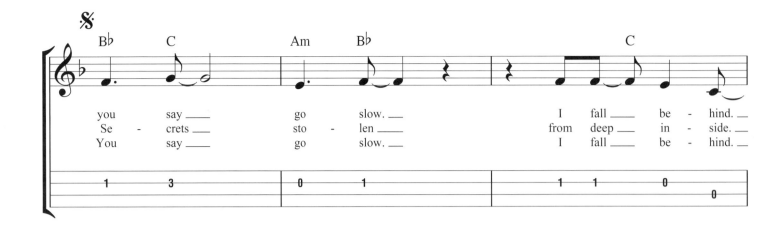

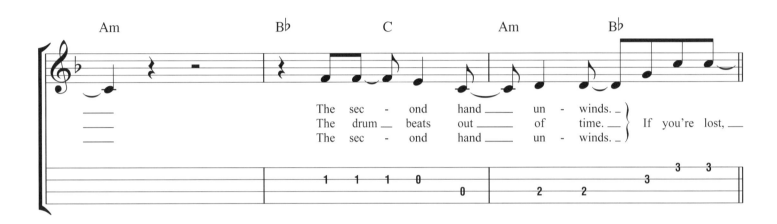

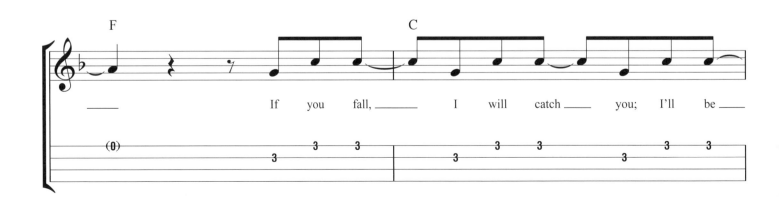

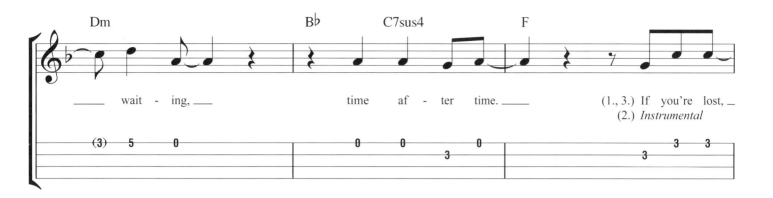

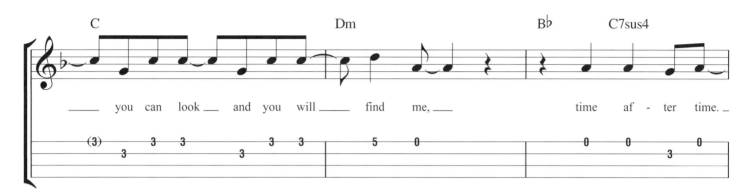

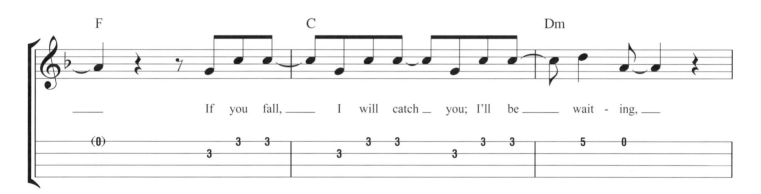

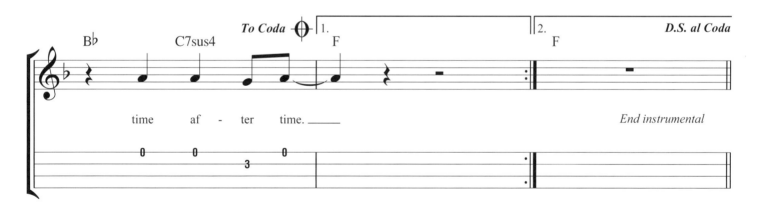

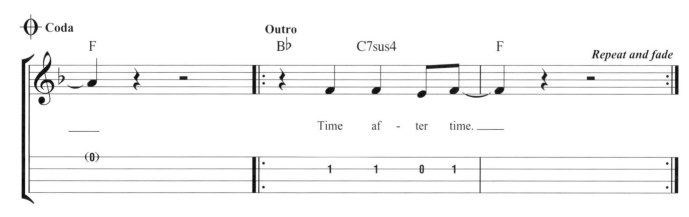

The Times They Are A-Changin'

Words and Music by Bob Dylan

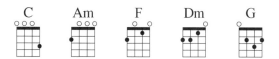

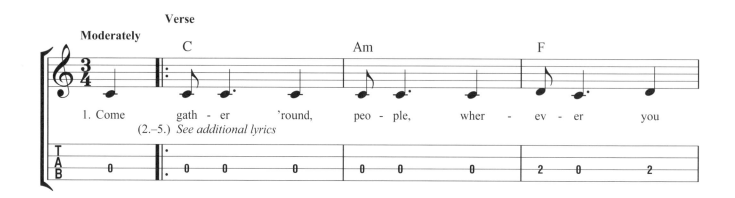

Verse

Moderately

1. Come gath - er 'round, peo - ple, wher - ev - er you

(2.–5.) *See additional lyrics*

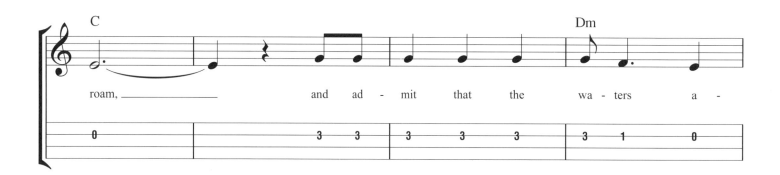

roam, _____ and ad - mit that the wa - ters a -

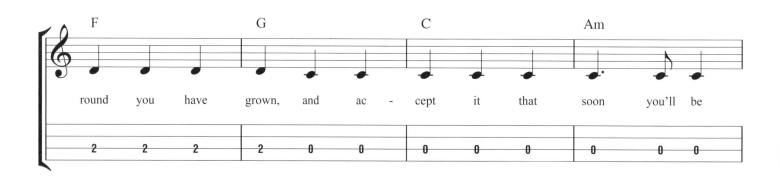

round you have grown, and ac - cept it that soon you'll be

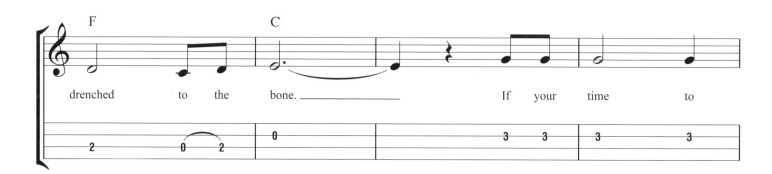

drenched to the bone. _____ If your time to

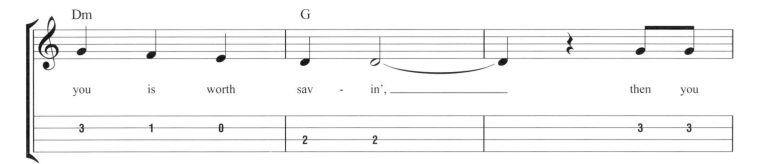

you   is   worth   sav - in', _____   then you

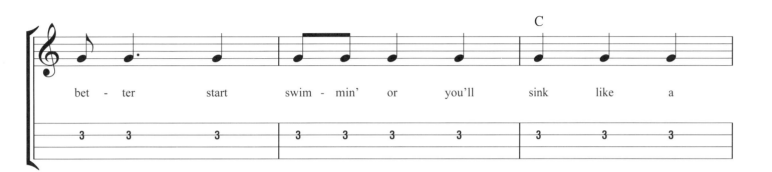

bet - ter   start   swim - min'   or   you'll   sink   like   a

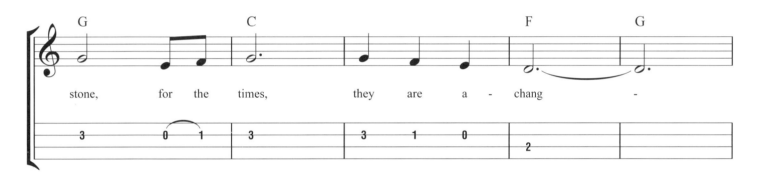

stone,   for   the   times,   they   are   a -   chang   -

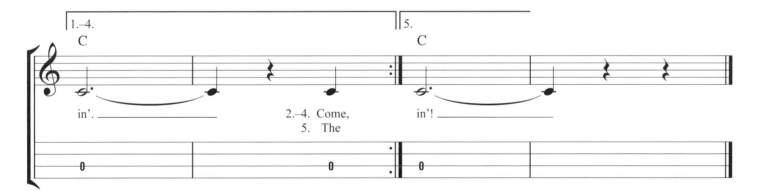

1.–4.

in'. _____   2.–4. Come,
                        5. The

5.

in'! _____

Additional Lyrics

2. Come, writers and critics who prophesy with your pen,
   And keep your eyes wide; the chance won't come again.
   And don't speak too soon, for the wheel's still in spin,
   And there's no tellin' who that it's namin'.
   For the loser now will be later to win,
   For the times, they are a-changin'.

3. Come, senators, congressmen, please heed the call.
   Don't stand in the doorway, don't block up the hall.
   For he that gets hurt will be he who has stalled.
   There's a battle outside and it's ragin'.
   It'll soon shake your windows and rattle your walls,
   For the times, they are a-changin'!

4. Come, mothers and fathers throughout the land,
   And don't criticize what you can't understand.
   Your sons and your daughters are beyond your command;
   Your old road is rapidly agin'.
   Please get out of the new one if you can't lend your hand,
   For the times, they are a-changin'!

5. The line it is drawn, the curse it is cast.
   The slow one now will later be fast.
   As the present now will later be past,
   The order is rapidly fadin'.
   And the first one now will later be last,
   For the times, they are a-changin'!

Vincent
(Starry Starry Night)

Words and Music by Don McLean

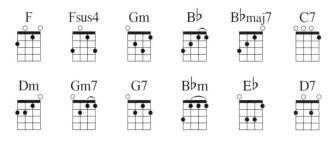

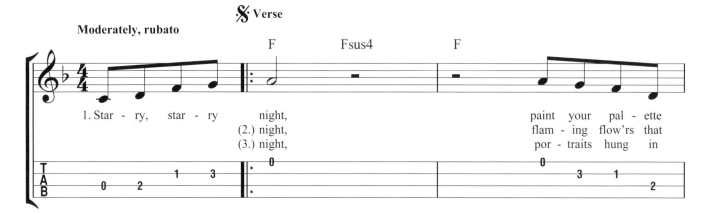

Moderately, rubato

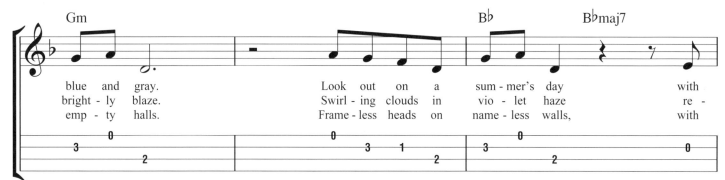

1. Star - ry, star - ry night, paint your pal - ette
(2.) night, flam - ing flow'rs that
(3.) night, por - traits hung in

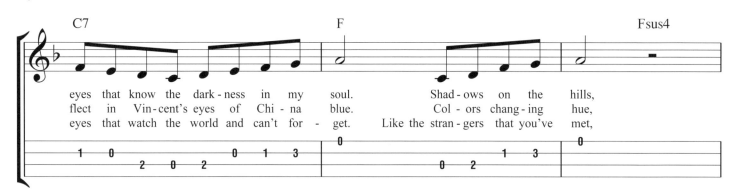

blue and gray. Look out on a sum - mer's day with
bright - ly blaze. Swirl - ing clouds in vio - let haze re -
emp - ty halls. Frame - less heads on name - less walls, with

eyes that know the dark - ness in my soul. Shad - ows on the hills,
flect in Vin - cent's eyes of Chi - na blue. Col - ors chang - ing hue,
eyes that watch the world and can't for - get. Like the stran - gers that you've met,

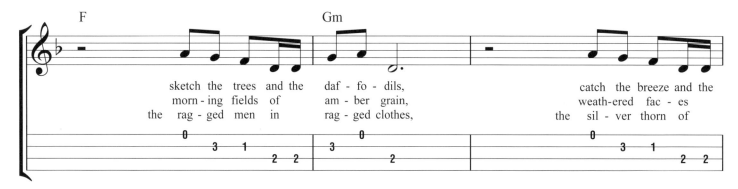

sketch the trees and the daf - fo - dils, catch the breeze and the
morn - ing fields of am - ber grain, weath-ered fac - es
the rag - ged men in rag - ged clothes, the sil - ver thorn of

winter chills in colors on the snow - y lin - en land.
lined in pain are soothed be - neath the art - ist's lov - ing hand.
blood - y rose, lie crushed and bro - ken on the vir - gin snow.

Chorus

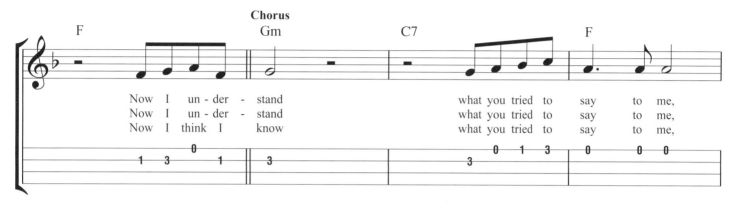

Now I un - der - stand what you tried to say to me,
Now I un - der - stand what you tried to say to me,
Now I think I know what you tried to say to me,

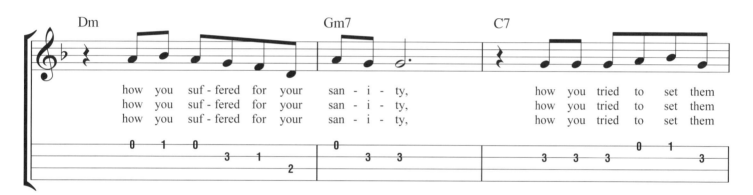

how you suf - fered for your san - i - ty, how you tried to set them
how you suf - fered for your san - i - ty, how you tried to set them
how you suf - fered for your san - i - ty, how you tried to set them

To Coda

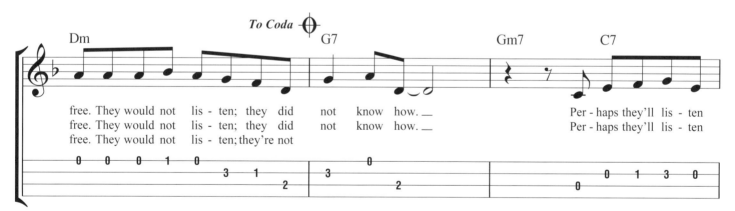

free. They would not lis - ten; they did not know how. __ Per - haps they'll lis - ten
free. They would not lis - ten; they did not know how. __ Per - haps they'll lis - ten
free. They would not lis - ten; they're not

1.

2.

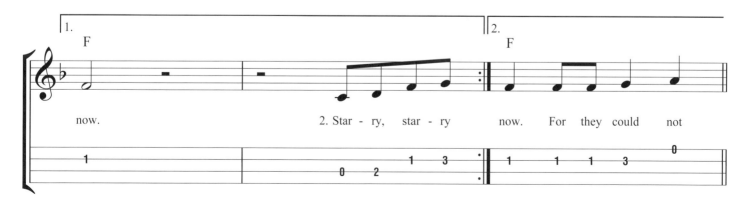

now.
now. 2. Star - ry, star - ry now. For they could not

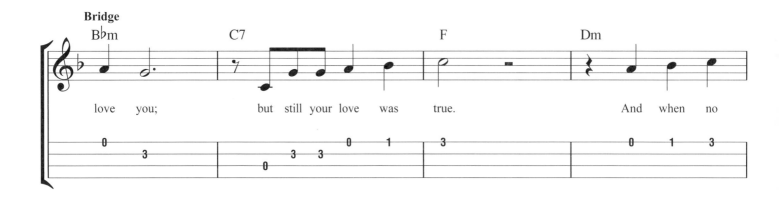

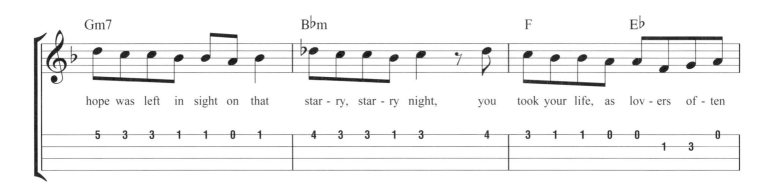

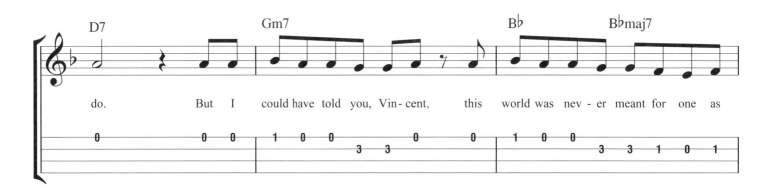

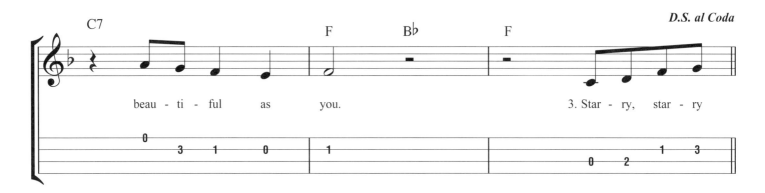

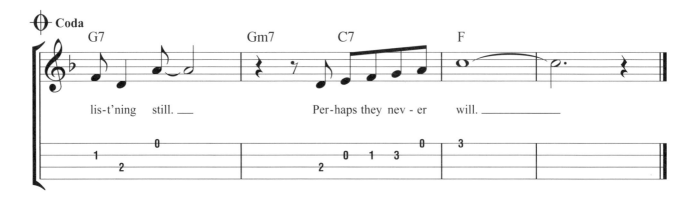

Take Me Home, Country Roads

Words and Music by John Denver, Bill Danoff and Taffy Nivert

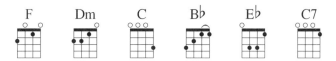

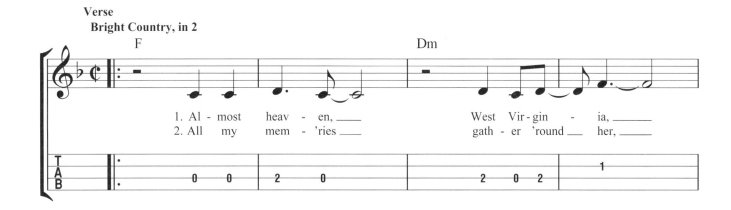

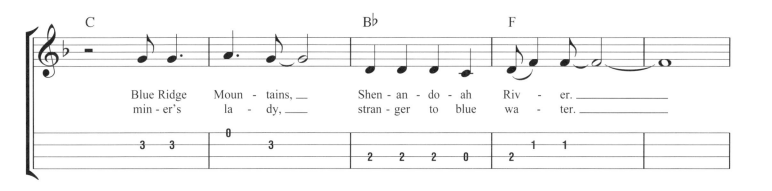

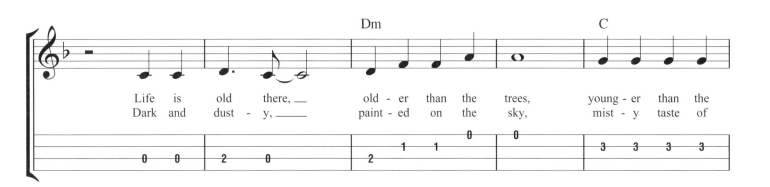

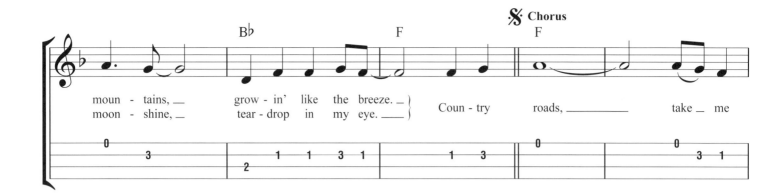

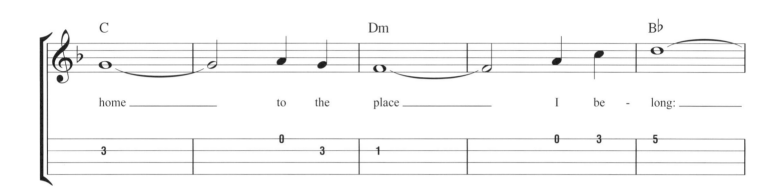

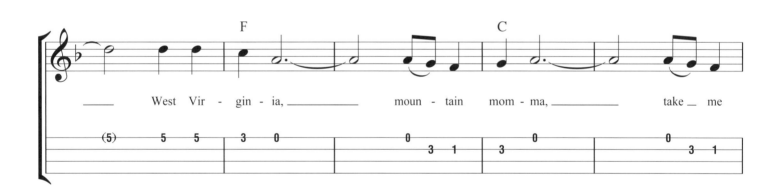

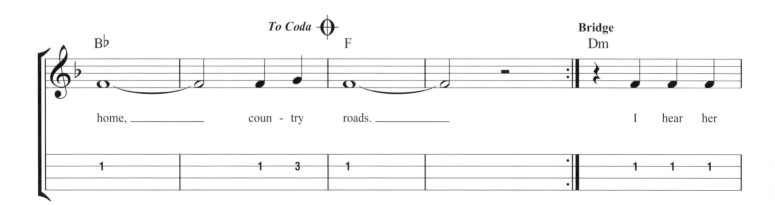

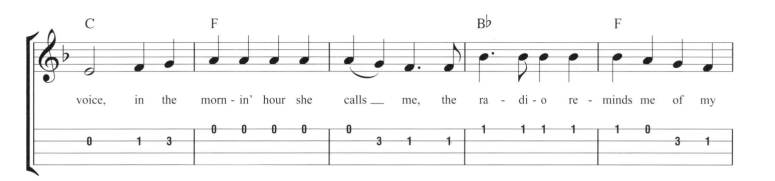

voice, in the morn-in' hour she calls ___ me, the ra-di-o re-minds me of my

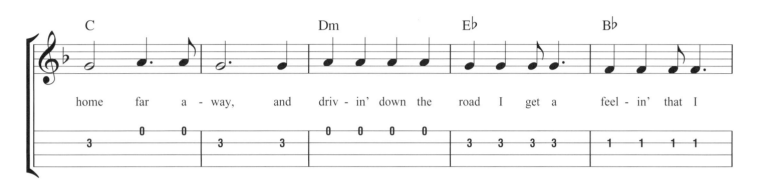

home far a-way, and driv-in' down the road I get a feel-in' that I

D.S. al Coda

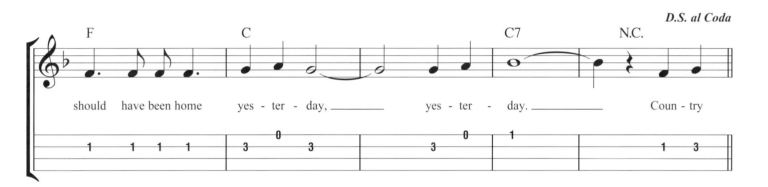

should have been home yes-ter-day, _____ yes-ter-day. _____ Coun-try

Coda   **Outro**

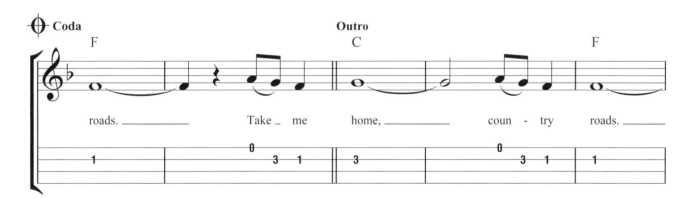

roads. _____ Take _ me home, _____ coun-try roads. _____

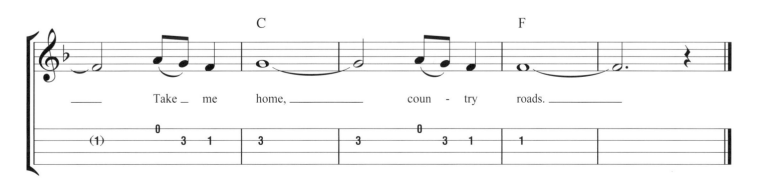

_____ Take _ me home, _____ coun-try roads. _____

We Shall Overcome

Musical Adaptation and Arrangement by Zilphia Horton, Frank Hamilton, Guy Carawan and Pete Seeger
Inspired by African American Gospel Singing, members of the Food and Tobacco Workers Union,
Charleston, SC, and the southern Civil Rights Movement

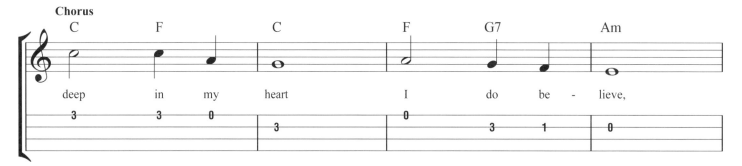

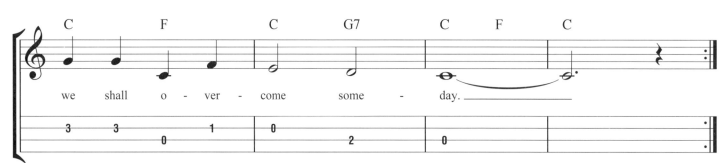

Additional Lyrics

3. We shall live in peace,
   We shall live in peace,
   We shall live in peace someday.

4. We shall all be free,
   We shall all be free,
   We shall all be free someday.

5. We are not afraid,
   We are not afraid,
   We are not afraid today.

When I Need You

Words and Music by Carole Bayer Sager and Albert Hammond

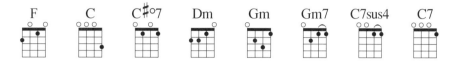

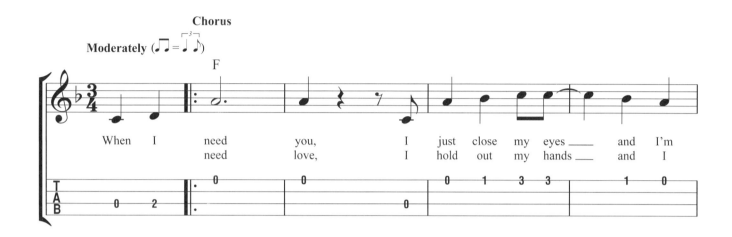

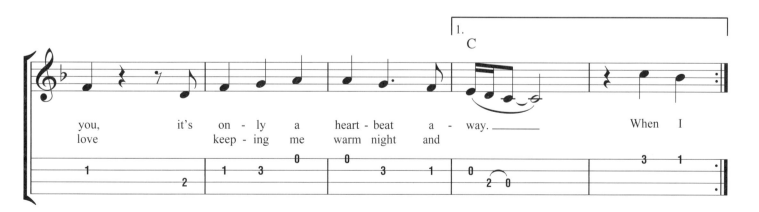

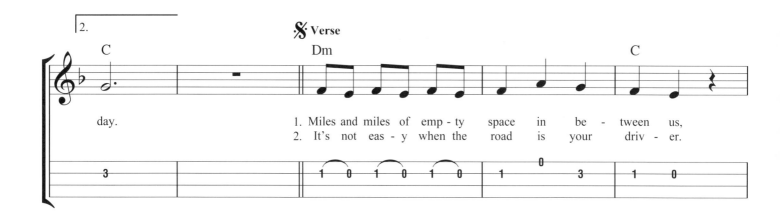

day.

1. Miles and miles of emp-ty space in be - tween us,
2. It's not eas-y when the road is your driv - er.

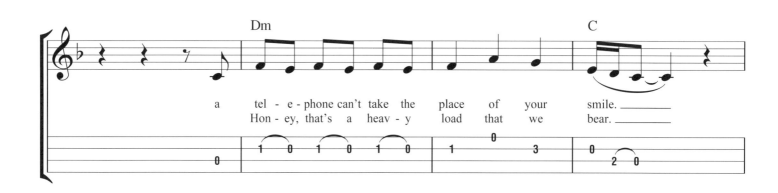

a tel - e - phone can't take the place of your smile. _____
Hon - ey, that's a heav - y load that we bear. _____

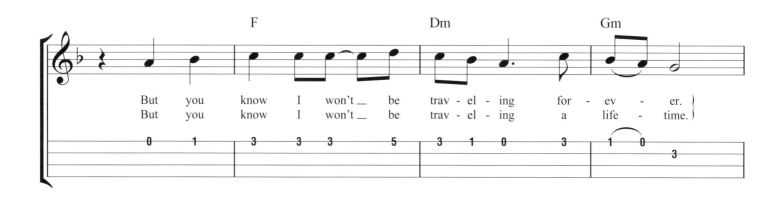

But you know I won't _ be trav - el - ing for - ev - er.
But you know I won't _ be trav - el - ing a life - time.

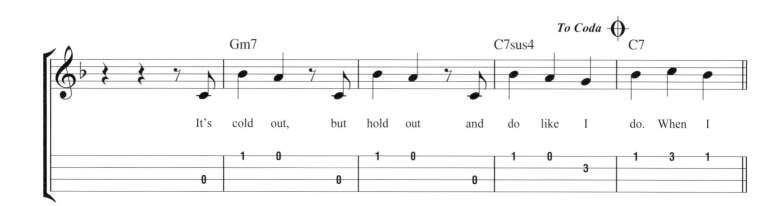

It's cold out, but hold out and do like I do. When I

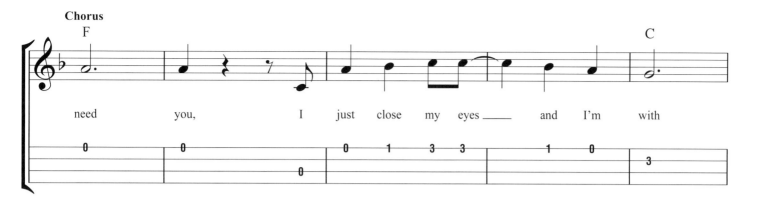

need you,   you,   I   just   close   my   eyes _____   and   I'm   with

you,   and   all   that   I   so   want   to   give   you,   babe,

it's   on - ly   a   heart - beat   a - way. _____

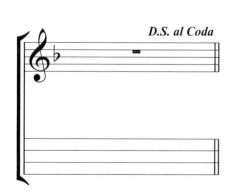

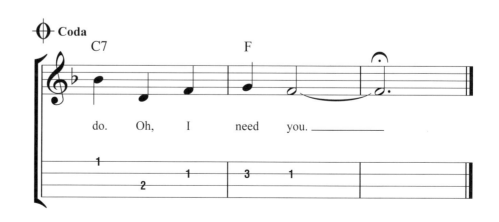

do.   Oh,   I   need   you. _____

What the World Needs Now Is Love

Lyric by Hal David
Music by Burt Bacharach

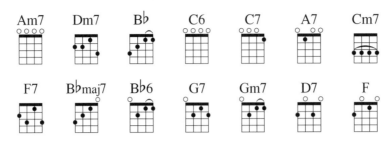

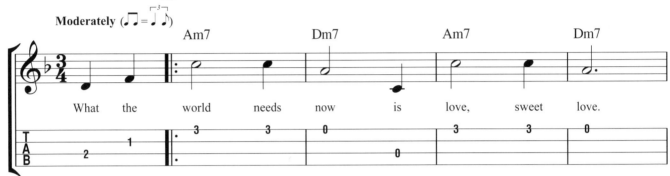

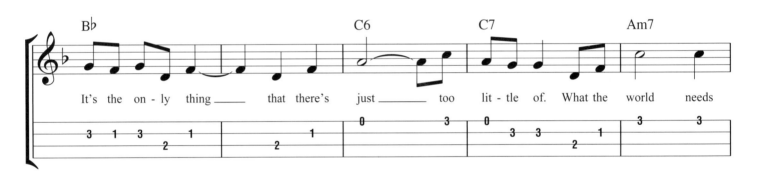

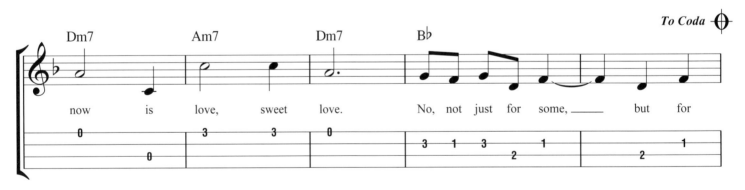

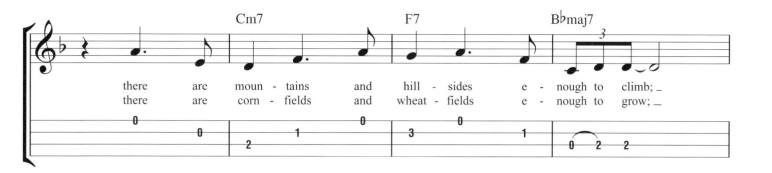

there are moun - tains and hill - sides e - nough to climb; _
there are corn - fields and wheat - fields e - nough to grow; _

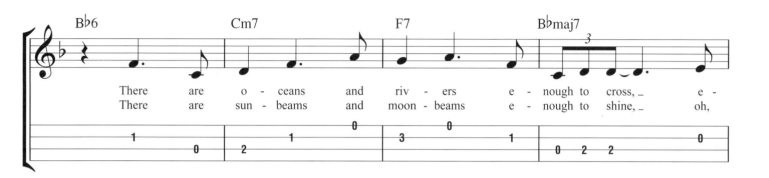

There are o - ceans and riv - ers e - nough to cross, _ e -
There are sun - beams and moon - beams e - nough to shine, _ oh,

2nd time, D.S. al Coda

nough to last, _ till the end of time. ⎫ What the
lis - ten, Lord, _ if you want to know. ⎭

Coda

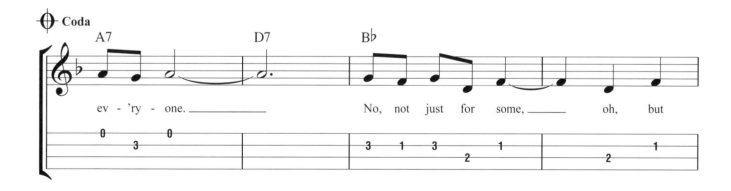

ev - 'ry - one. _____ No, not just for some, _____ oh, but

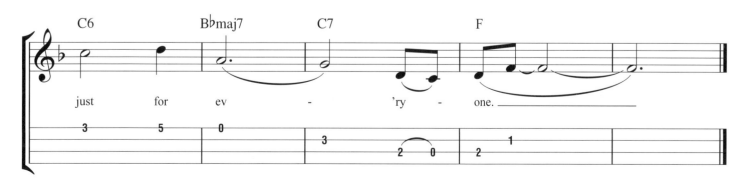

just for ev - 'ry - one. _____

99

You Are My Sunshine

Words and Music by Jimmie Davis

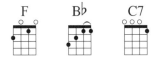

F   Bb   C7

Verse

Lively, in 2

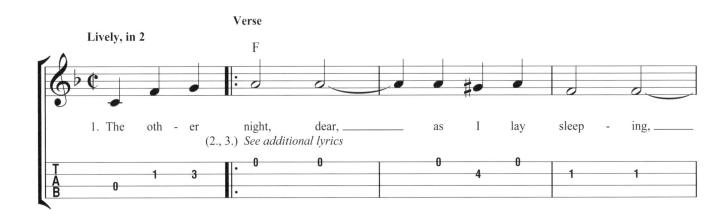

1. The oth - er night, dear, _____ as I lay sleep - ing, _____
(2., 3.) *See additional lyrics*

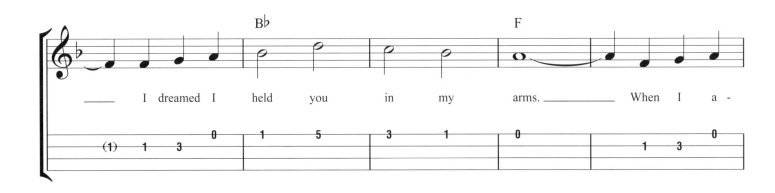

_____ I dreamed I held you in my arms. _____ When I a -

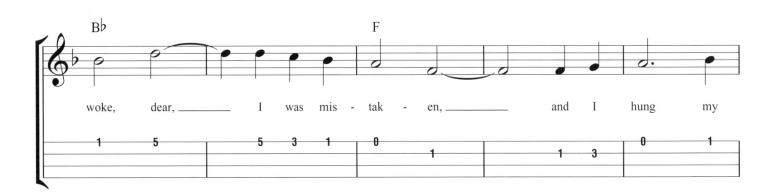

woke, dear, _____ I was mis - tak - en, _____ and I hung my

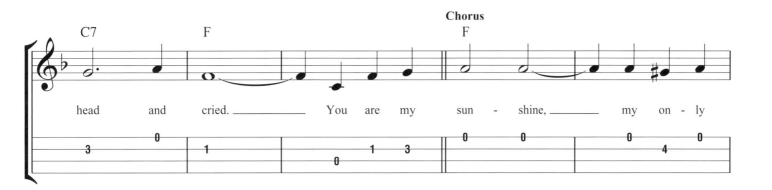

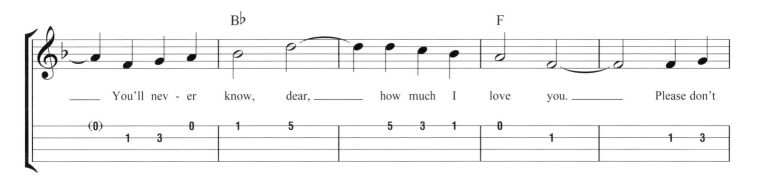

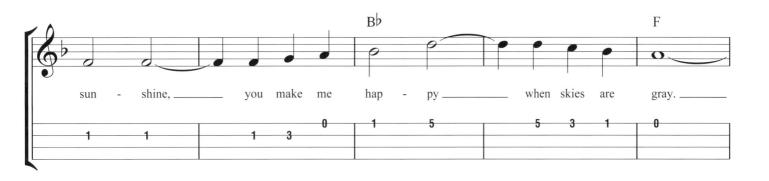

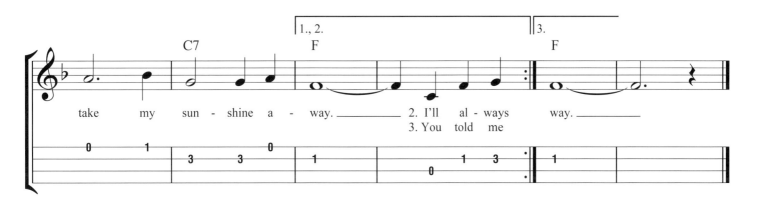

Additional Lyrics

2. I'll always love you and make you happy
If you will only say the same.
But if you leave me to love another,
You'll regret it all someday.

3. You told me once, dear, you really loved me
And no one else could come between.
But now you've left me and love another;
You have shattered all my dreams.

When the Saints Go Marching In

Words by Katherine E. Purvis
Music by James M. Black

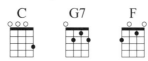

Moderately bright, in 2

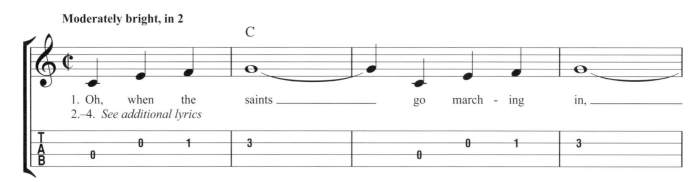

1. Oh, when the saints _____ go march - ing in, _____
2.–4. *See additional lyrics*

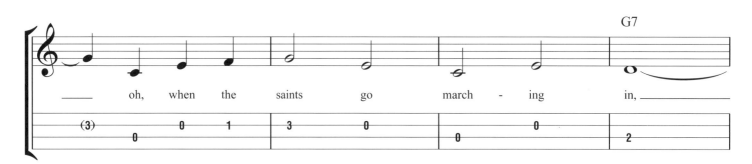

_____ oh, when the saints go march - ing in, _____

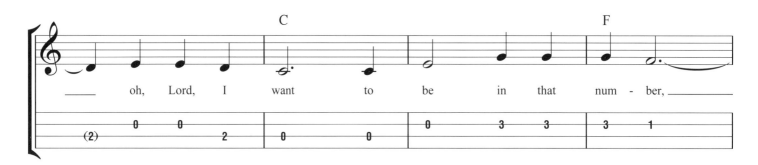

_____ oh, Lord, I want to be in that num - ber, _____

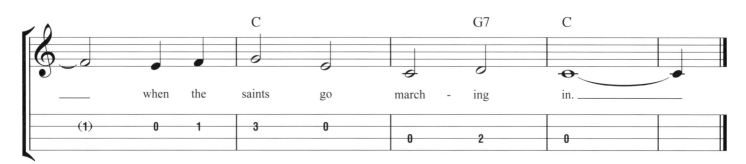

_____ when the saints go march - ing in.

Additional Lyrics

2. Oh, when the sun refuse to shine,
Oh, when the sun refuse to shine,
Oh, Lord, I want to be in that number,
When the sun refuse to shine.

3. Oh, when the stars have disappeared,
Oh, when the stars have disappeared,
Oh, Lord, I want to be in that number,
When the stars have disappeared.

4. Oh, when the day of judgment comes,
Oh, when the day of judgment comes,
Oh, Lord, I want to be in that number,
When the day of judgment comes.

UKULELE ENSEMBLE SERIES

The songs in these collections are playable by any combination of ukuleles (soprano, concert, tenor or baritone). Each arrangement features the melody, a harmony part, and a "bass" line. Chord symbols are also provided if you wish to add a rhythm part. For groups with more than three or four ukuleles, the parts may be doubled.

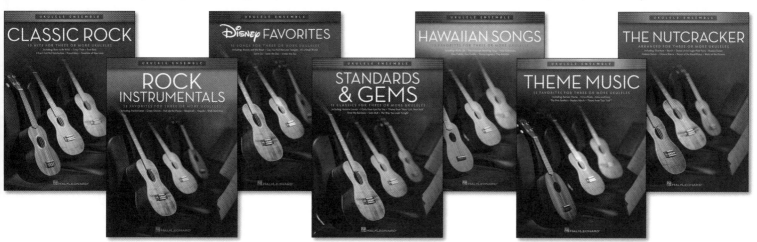

THE BEATLES
Mid-Intermediate Level

All My Loving • Blackbird • Can't Buy Me Love • Eight Days a Week • Here, There and Everywhere • I Want to Hold Your Hand • Let It Be • Love Me Do • Norwegian Wood (This Bird Has Flown) • Penny Lane • Something • Ticket to Ride • When I'm Sixty-Four • Yellow Submarine • Yesterday.
00295927 .... $9.99

CHRISTMAS SONGS
Early Intermediate Level

The Chipmunk Song • The Christmas Song (Chestnuts Roasting on an Open Fire) • Do You Hear What I Hear • Feliz Navidad • Frosty the Snow Man • Have Yourself a Merry Little Christmas • Here Comes Santa Claus (Right Down Santa Claus Lane) • A Holly Jolly Christmas • (There's No Place Like) Home for the Holidays • Jingle Bell Rock • The Little Drummer Boy • Merry Christmas, Darling • The Most Wonderful Time of the Year • Silver Bells • White Christmas.
00129247 .... $9.99

CLASSIC ROCK
Mid-Intermediate Level

Aqualung • Behind Blue Eyes • Born to Be Wild • Crazy Train • Fly Like an Eagle • Free Bird • Hey Jude • Low Rider • Moondance • Oye Como Va • Proud Mary • (I Can't Get No) Satisfaction • Smoke on the Water • Summertime Blues • Sunshine of Your Love.
00103904 .... $10.99

DISNEY FAVORITES
Early Intermediate Level

The Bare Necessities • Beauty and the Beast • Can You Feel the Love Tonight • Colors of the Wind • A Dream Is a Wish Your Heart Makes • It's a Small World • Let It Go • Let's Go Fly a Kite • Little April Shower • Mickey Mouse March • Seize the Day • The Siamese Cat Song • Supercalifragilisticexpialidocious • Under the Sea • A Whole New World.
00279513 .... $9.99

HAWAIIAN SONGS
Mid-Intermediate Level

Aloha Oe • Beyond the Rainbow • Harbor Lights • Hawaiian War Chant (Ta-Hu-Wa-Hu-Wai) • The Hawaiian Wedding Song (Ke Kali Nei Au) • Ka-lu-a • Lovely Hula Hands • Mele Kalikimaka • The Moon of Manakoora • One Paddle, Two Paddle • Pearly Shells (Pupu 'O 'Ewa) • Red Sails in the Sunset • Sleepy Lagoon • Song of the Islands • Tiny Bubbles.
00119254 .... $9.99

THE NUTCRACKER
Late Intermediate Level

Arabian Dance ("Coffee") • Chinese Dance ("Tea") • Dance of the Reed-Flutes • Dance of the Sugar Plum Fairy • March • Overture • Russian Dance ("Trepak") • Waltz of the Flowers.
00119908 .... $9.99

ROCK INSTRUMENTALS
Late Intermediate Level

Beck's Bolero • Cissy Strut • Europa (Earth's Cry Heaven's Smile) • Frankenstein • Green Onions • Jessica • Misirlou • Perfidia • Pick Up the Pieces • Pipeline • Rebel 'Rouser • Sleepwalk • Tequila • Walk Don't Run • Wipe Out.
00103909 .... $9.99

STANDARDS & GEMS
Mid-Intermediate Level

Autumn Leaves • Cheek to Cheek • Easy to Love • Fly Me to the Moon • I Only Have Eyes for You • It Had to Be You • Laura • Mack the Knife • My Funny Valentine • Theme from "New York, New York" • Over the Rainbow • Satin Doll • Some Day My Prince Will Come • Summertime • The Way You Look Tonight.
00103898 .... $9.99

THEME MUSIC
Mid-Intermediate Level

Batman Theme • Theme from E.T. (The Extra-Terrestrial) • Forrest Gump – Main Title (Feather Theme) • The Godfather (Love Theme) • Hawaii Five-O Theme • He's a Pirate • Linus and Lucy • Mission: Impossible Theme • Peter Gunn • The Pink Panther • Raiders March • (Ghost) Riders in the Sky (A Cowboy Legend) • Theme from Spider Man • Theme from "Star Trek®" • Theme from "Superman."
00103903 .... $10.99

www.halleonard.com

Prices, contents, and availability subject to change without notice.

Disney Characters and Artwork TM & © 2019 Disney

Hal•Leonard® UKULELE PLAY-ALONG

Now you can play your favorite songs on your uke with great-sounding backing tracks to help you sound like a bona fide pro! The audio also features playback tools so you can adjust the tempo without changing the pitch and loop challenging parts.

1. POP HITS
00701451 Book/CD Pack $15.99

3. HAWAIIAN FAVORITES
00701453 Book/Online Audio........... $14.99

4. CHILDREN'S SONGS
00701454 Book/Online Audio........... $14.99

5. CHRISTMAS SONGS
00701696 Book/CD Pack $12.99

6. LENNON & MCCARTNEY
00701723 Book/Online Audio........... $12.99

7. DISNEY FAVORITES
00701724 Book/Online Audio........... $14.99

8. CHART HITS
00701745 Book/CD Pack $15.99

9. THE SOUND OF MUSIC
00701784 Book/CD Pack $14.99

10. MOTOWN
00701964 Book/CD Pack $12.99

11. CHRISTMAS STRUMMING
00702458 Book/Online Audio........... $12.99

12. BLUEGRASS FAVORITES
00702584 Book/CD Pack $12.99

13. UKULELE SONGS
00702599 Book/CD Pack $12.99

14. JOHNNY CASH
00702615 Book/Online Audio........... $15.99

15. COUNTRY CLASSICS
00702834 Book/CD Pack $12.99

16. STANDARDS
00702835 Book/CD Pack $12.99

17. POP STANDARDS
00702836 Book/CD Pack $12.99

18. IRISH SONGS
00703086 Book/Online Audio........... $12.99

19. BLUES STANDARDS
00703087 Book/CD Pack $12.99

20. FOLK POP ROCK
00703088 Book/CD Pack $12.99

21. HAWAIIAN CLASSICS
00703097 Book/CD Pack $12.99

22. ISLAND SONGS
00703098 Book/CD Pack $12.99

23. TAYLOR SWIFT
00221966 Book/Online Audio........... $16.99

24. WINTER WONDERLAND
00101871 Book/CD Pack $12.99

25. GREEN DAY
00110398 Book/CD Pack $14.99

26. BOB MARLEY
00110399 Book/Online Audio........... $14.99

27. TIN PAN ALLEY
00116358 Book/CD Pack $12.99

28. STEVIE WONDER
00116736 Book/CD Pack $14.99

29. OVER THE RAINBOW & OTHER FAVORITES
00117076 Book/Online Audio........... $15.99

30. ACOUSTIC SONGS
00122336 Book/CD Pack $14.99

31. JASON MRAZ
00124166 Book/CD Pack $14.99

32. TOP DOWNLOADS
00127507 Book/CD Pack $14.99

33. CLASSICAL THEMES
00127892 Book/Online Audio........... $14.99

34. CHRISTMAS HITS
00128602 Book/CD Pack $14.99

35. SONGS FOR BEGINNERS
00129009 Book/Online Audio........... $14.99

36. ELVIS PRESLEY HAWAII
00138199 Book/Online Audio........... $14.99

37. LATIN
00141191 Book/Online Audio........... $14.99

38. JAZZ
00141192 Book/Online Audio........... $14.99

39. GYPSY JAZZ
00146559 Book/Online Audio........... $15.99

40. TODAY'S HITS
00160845 Book/Online Audio........... $14.99

HAL•LEONARD®

www.halleonard.com

Prices, contents, and availability subject to change without notice.